The Girl Who Found Water

Memoirs of a Corps member

Chibuzor Mirian Azubuike

hello@chibuzorazubuike.com
www.chibuzorazubuike.com
Instagram: chibuzor_azubuike

+2348061258783

First Edition: October 2014
Second Edition : August 2021

Edited by Kenechi Uzochukwu

ISBN 978-978-943-957-7

DEDICATION

To all National Youth Service Corps Members in the
past, present and future

TABLE OF CONTENTS

ACKNOWLEDGEMENT

Special thanks to His Excellency, Mallam Dr Isa Yuguda, Governor of Bauchi state and to the Bauchi State Director, State Security Service, Mr Tosin Ajayi. Thanks also to Ishola Micheal. I appreciate my parents Hyacinth and Jane Azubuike, my lovely brothers Obinna, Kenechukwu and Chinedu Azubuike for propel- ling me to Succeed. Thanks to Kenneth Azubuike, and all the Azubuikes, Obiegbus, Morahs, Udezes and Chimas.

Many thanks to you, Kenechi Uzochukwu, my brilliant and strict Editor. I also want to appreciate all my supportive friends: Onosedeba Imoloame, Sophia Momoh, Idahosa Sammy, Martins Ezuma, Nkemchor Jeremiah, Ope Great Awoyode, Paul Orude, Artu Markus and Martins Okafor. Esther Mark, Francis Ezeweani, Chibuzor Okere, Margaret Okorojokwu,

Thank you. Thanks also to Okechukwu Ofili, Onyeka Nwelue and Matt Whyman for your constructive criticisms.

I thank the NYSC scheme, MDGs Advocacy Project, Management and Staff of Bauchi State Television, the people of Bauchi and the community of Bigi Tudunwada. God bless Nigeria.

Chibuzor Mirian Azubuike

FOREWORD

Chibuzor Azubuike, one corps member who made the difference with her passion to touch the lives of her host community in Bauchi State where she was posted to serve has captured the dilemma most corps members posted to serve in the north east face, in a style that gives simplicity, freshness and powerful narration. She focuses on the difficult decision making moment of the corps member posted to ‗war‘ states‘ in the north east using her story to capture the confusion that agitates minds of graduates posted to Bauchi.

The heat of the killing of nine corps members in the state had not petered down when she received her posting to Bauchi. She summed up the attendant frustration by towing the paths most people in her situation would do: redeploy immediately. The turmoil that greeted the posting of a typical Lagosian‘ to the north, as examined in this book has been used by the author to expose the unsubstantiated stories of how unpleasant the region could be for corps members.

What we are dealing with invariably are the following issues: ignorance or little knowledge of the history, culture and traditions of other Nigerians: there is a deep prejudice attached to other ethnic groups. The failure of Nigerians to embrace one another has continued to be an impediment to success of the NYSC scheme and the overall unity of the country. Under the current state of things, corps members are no longer attracted to adopt where they are posted to serve as their home.

The role of the NYSC: This book documents the efforts of the scheme over the years to address some of the seemingly over- whelming problems of integrating the scheme and puts special value of the contributions of the thousands of corps members posted yearly to serve across the country. It still gives us a picture of an organised effort to sustain the programme in spite of the difficulty by galvanising the youths who execute numerous community projects which in turn have direct bearing on the host communi- ties.

The role of the state government: Even though the NYSC scheme is a federal government project, the states have a responsibility to support the corps members posted to their states by ensuring their welfare and security is guaranteed. The various states governments can do a lot to make the scheme attractive by providing employment opportunities for the corps members that served in their states. Besides taking them from the labour market, such corps members can become the drive to aid development in such states.

The author's style is entertaining and captivating and shows prospect of becoming a writer that would give the reader a lot to be thankful for if she churn out more works like this. Giving a vivid picture of the drama that followed her discovery that she had been posted to Bauchi (her reaction was unexpectedly dramatic and interesting), she made inquiries which further produced mixed feelings, and with assurances that Bauchi was not a bad place, she made the journey into an unexpected and perhaps initially unwanted adventure. Before her sojourn, she constructs the narratives in a sequence and takes us into the reactions that greet such postings.

She provides us with a broad picture of the little knowledge of the average Nigerian about his country as she takes us through her journey to the north and her eventual arrival at the orientation camp in Wailo. The strength of her narrative ability is well captured about the 'culture shock' she experienced even while in camp. The author took time to give a good account of her experience which is a must read for corps members posted not just to the north but any part of the country. She made us see that because we have little or no knowledge about our country, we rely on half-truths and sometimes lies from other people.

But this is a work of a soldier who had been to the battle field, with a spark of passion to change lives. The author has been able to produce the lessons we can learn from failing to know about our country. She was shedding tears because she was posted to Bauchi State but after six months, she was offered redeployment but buoyed by the need to make impact on the lives of the less privileged, the author was not willing to leave until her purpose was fulfilled. Not only did her project touch the lives of the people, she left Bauchi as a heroine and her name was immortalised.

It is indeed a thing of treasure that the author put down her experience in the written word, indeed an avenue for future intervention. She has written this book at an auspicious time in the history of the country. While Boko Haram continues to kill innocent citizens, there has been growing fears that corps members should not be posted to affected states. Bauchi has been fortunate to be free from insurgency but the stigma that it is susceptible to Boko Haram has made many parents and guardians from the southern part of the country not to welcome the idea of allowing their children to travel to Bauchi or the north to serve. The author has demonstrated that all is not lost. With the adequate knowledge of others, passion and determination, corps members from the south posted to the north to serve should see it as a call to duty, to serve fatherland and be patriotic enough to accept and in- deed conceive ideas, projects that they would execute that would make impact in the lives of the people they are called to serve.

Mallam Dr. Isa Yuguda, Governor of Bauchi state

THE BIG NEWS

The day broke and I watched as it gathered itself up. Between the sounds of the ticking clock I heard lives stirring up abroad. I heard the cockcrows too. They were distinct: the one with the low crow must be the Agric-breed (my father called them "bread soaked in water," because they were so big, yet so weak), and the well-stressed crows were from Mama Bose's poultry.

I had been looking forward to this day: the day I would finally get to rest after compiling the pupils end of term results. I quickly showered and headed to the school before my boss, the head mistress, would flog me with her eyes. Her scornful look at an erring teacher and her harsh words could make someone wet themselves. You dared not call her by her name, or "Aunty" – you must call her "Mummy HM" or "Mummy." Before now I thought that "Mummy" was a title reserved exclusively for that woman who carried you in her womb for nine months, who went through the hurdles of childbirth, who went through great pains to have you. However, it was a common trend in this part of the world to call any woman who was old enough to be your mother "Mummy". It was a sign of respect.

It was the period children go to school happily, knowing the holidays were drawing closer. Enough time to play, no more *bend your head on the table*, *stop making noise*, no more teachers' screams, no more ringing bells. Parents weren't looking forward to the holidays; it would be their turn to scream, as my mum did in those good old days when I was a child. *"You children should not go out to play rough o…My God, who injured you? See, you children can't kill me o. My mother had nine children but she is still alive, I have just four".*

The children on my street were also going to school. "Mummy, buy me *bobo*." The little boy was pointing to *Iya* Jide's shop. *Iya* Jide, who was in her late seventies, opened her shop at 6:30 every morning so she wouldn't miss the school children pointing to her shop crying that their parents should buy them *bobo*. She was always happy during school term because it meant more profit.

I was sure some poor parents wished *Iya* Jide didn't wake up so early to open her shop. *Iya* Jide was short and possessed a very loud voice: she would never need a microphone to speak to a crowd of people. She shouted *ekaro o* to anyone passing by to catch their attention. Her shop was busy in the mornings but she still noticed everyone walking past. She would greet you in the morning with a smile, moving her body as though she were dancing, continuously untying and tying the wrapper at her chest, revealing her sagging breasts. Sometimes she tied the wrapper on her waist and wore an old black bra. *If Iya Jide was educated she would have been a seasoned marketer and would pay attention to her dressing,* I often thought. She knew how to arrange her goods in such a way that one could not help but to look into her shop. She had a long shelf on which she put sweets of the same kind together. She always bought the ones that had colorful wrappers. She arranged the drinks by size; the smallest ones she kept at the bottom of the shelf, while the biggest ones were at the top.

"*Ekaro* Mirian," she waved at me. I knew she was not just greeting me.

"*Ekaro* ma," I responded. "Sell well o."

3

"Okay o, thank you o!" That was the best I could do for her: I had rice and stew in my flask which I would have for breakfast at the 11: 00am break time. I got to school at 7:30, wrote my name in the teachers' register and headed straight to the chapel where all the teachers said our special morning prayers at 7:45. At 8: 00am we would join the pupils on the assembly ground.

Just before I entered the chapel my phone rang. It was Sophia.

"Hello, Sophia how are you doing, and how is Benin?"

"Hello Mirian. Benin is fine. Clearance has started. And you have to come today to do your clearance. Also, the Call-up letter will soon be out, oh!"

"Today?"

"Yes, Today. The clearance is likely to end tomorrow."

"Hmmn." Ok, thanks for the info. I will head for Benin straight away."

Now I had to face the tedious task of telling Mummy HM that I had to travel immediately. I was only teaching at the school to prevent idleness while I waited to receive my Posting letter and learn where I would be serving my fatherland. I had taught there for three months making the necessary income, because my father believed that after paying our school fees, he owed his children nothing more. When I finished my final exams, I had to get a job that paid something, no matter how small. Being a teacher was a very exciting experience. I had never taught before, but my pupils were very cooperative and intelligent. Although I suffered incessant headaches, I still enjoyed every bit of the job. I had to summon courage to tell Mummy HM that I would be leaving for Benin immediately. If I hesitated and didn't leave that day, I might not make the June batch and would then be posted for service in November. Even though I enjoyed teaching my pupils, I definitely did not want to teach them till November.

"Good morning Mummy, I just got an urgent call from the university that I should travel immediately to do my clearance. Please ma, I have to go to Benin now."

I acted out the drama well. I panted and delivered my message in a life and death manner. Her face changed.

"Hmmm…can't you go tomorrow?"

"Tomorrow is Friday, ma. If I get there on Friday, it would be late – school does not open on the weekends and I might have to wait till Monday, and Mummy, from the way my friend delivered the message, it must be an emergency."

"Alright, then hand over the results to another teacher. I wish you a safe journey."

"Thank you Mummy, God bless you."

I sighed in relief. My acting must have been good.

I immediately rushed home, put a few clothes in a small bag and rushed to the ATM to withdraw the salary I had been saving up for emergencies. I headed straight to Mile 2park where I knew I would get a bus to Benin even at noon. I was lucky to be the thirteenth person on the fifteen-seat bus; just two more passengers and we would be on our way to Benin.

My hopes were high that my dreams would finally come true. I knew that I would definitely not be posted to any state in northern Nigeria; I would be posted to the south-south – or even the south-west. My joy was overflowing.

We left the Mile 2Park at 1pm. I knew we would get to Benin late and that the bad roads would make the journey worse, but that did not stop my excitement. The driver out-maneuvered the traffic and we were soon on the Lagos-Ibadan expressway. Whenever I travelled, I preferred to sit by a window so that I could freely look outside and see the addresses on the signboards and know where we were. I always liked to be in the know. But this time I had gotten to the park late and the seats close to the windows were occupied. Nevertheless, I was carried away by my thoughts: I would be posted to a good state; I would work hard to get a job there because Lagos was overcrowded, and I would learn a foreign language like French or Spanish (or even both). I wouldn't have a child to disturb me, or my younger ones to remind me to make lunch. I was very happy that I had finally graduated from school. My department was the kind that when you graduated, you could throw a big party to celebrate. I was so excited: I would get my NYSC certificate which would enable me get a good job, buy a car, and live in the world of my dreams. I would go on vacations to any country of my choice; I would save and spend wisely.

"Buy banana, buy corn, sweet oranges." The highway hawkers, young and old, were beckoning on us as they ran toward our windows, hustling for their daily bread.

"Give me Fanta." I said to a teenage boy who handed me the chilled Fanta and I drank to chill my brain which I had stressed by fantasizing.

We were gradually approaching Ore where most drivers stopped to eat. There were many restaurants there, but the drivers usually stopped at one where they would be given free lunch so long as they brought their passengers. The passengers, after seating on the bus for hours, would be so tired that they would buy at the restaurant at which the driver stopped rather than find another one. I never liked to eat from those restaurants which often upset my stomach; I would rather buy bananas. There were always big, attractive bananas at Ore which were very affordable too. I wouldn't have had the courage to tell the driver to stop because I wanted to answer the call of nature. After twenty minutes the driver finished eating. He blew the horn to alert the rest of the passengers who went to eat at different places to board the bus so that we could continue our journey.

Less than an hour after we continued our journey, I began to feel as though I was already in Benin City. Maybe it was because the driver stopped playing Yoruba songs and started playing Bini music, or maybe it was because as I looked out of the window I saw red soil rather than brown. I went back to the world of my fantasies. I knew I was not there yet, but I loved the woman I was becoming. My friends always described me as strong-willed and ambitious. I could imagine myself in that dream office giving orders; someone helping me to carry my bag, opening my car door as I sit in the owner's corner…I kept smiling to myself. It was then I realized a lady seated close by had been staring at me, probably wondering if I was in the early stage of madness. She wouldn't understand: I was almost there and I was unstoppable. What more could I ask for? I had a whole year to develop myself.

At 6pm we got to Benin. It was too late to go to school, so I went to stay with my cousin, Ngozi, who lived adjacent to the university. Sophia, my closest friend, lived very far away and I did not want to risk going to her house that night. The next morning I got to school very early so that I would be the first person to be attended to. However, there were already lots of people waiting, but thanks to Sophia for informing me in good time, I finished my clearance and soon went to her place.

How times flies: we were once students, now we were graduates waiting to serve our fatherland for a year before we would eventually get jobs. Our expectations were higher than the clouds. Two days passed, and the list stating where we were posted was not out. I was anxious as my friends at other universities had been calling to tell me where they had been posted. When next the phone rang, I reached frantically for my phone only to discover it wasn't mine ringing but Sophia's. The list was out. Her former roommate was at school and had checked our names. This was the moment we had been waiting for. My heart beat faster, I was about to learn my fate.

"Where was I posted to?" Sophia listened, and shouted, "Thank God it is Delta! And Mirian, where was she posted to?" She did not again shout in excitement.

"Tell me please, what did she say?" I interrupted before she ended the call.

"Please calm down."

"Just tell me please, what did she say?" I didn't know if Sophia wanted to take her time to give me the news like doctors do when announcing the death of a patient to the relatives.

"What did she say? Where was I posted to?"

"Bauchi."

"Jesus! No, no, no! Not me, it is a lie!" I began to cry. My heart wanted to burst out of my mouth. I felt like the castle of my dreams had been crushed. I never imagined that I would be posted to such a place; I was not prepared for this. My depression began that day.

DILEMMA

I could not believe it. The terrible news hit me hard, too hard. I had high expectations, lofty dreams. And I had been so sure, so comfortable that my dreams would come true. I could almost touch it.

And then it all got shattered in an instant. Just like that.

Where was God? I had so much faith and optimism that I hadn't considered a plan B. Isn't that what one was supposed to do: to have faith and believe and not think or plan for the negative and unwanted?

Why did God not prove Himself in this situation, when all my hopes rested on him? I did not have a clue as to His *modus operandi* in answering prayers. I thought He was the helper of the helpless, the hope of the hopeless; that He never disappointed those who trusted in Him. I could not understand why He could not answer my simple prayer when He could raise the dead, heal the sick, and perform other mind-blowing miracles. Maybe He did not like me; maybe He wanted me to experience this pain. But if He knew me more than I know myself, then He should know that this pain was too excruciating for me to bear – I just couldn't take it anymore.

My eyes were heavy; the tears kept flowing like water from a fountain – I had no control over them anymore. It was as though I had been given news of the death of a family member. I felt frail and ill. Holding my umpteenth cup of water that day, eating was the last thing on my mind. Depression had set in. *Please*, I pleaded, *let someone wake me up to tell me it was a dream. This could not be happening.*

How could I be posted to Bauchi, a state in northern Nigeria for my mandatory national service after graduation? I wanted to learn a foreign language and engage in meaningful activities that would add to my CV and increase my chances of getting a good job after the mandatory service year, or maybe even remain wherever I was posted. But it was now impossible. These dreams were not the kinds that would be met in a place like Bauchi. This was a state where just two months ago, it was in the news that ten corps members were killed during post-election violence.

I will not go to Bauchi; I will never go to Bauchi. My heart was burning; what I usually felt as a heartbeat now felt like a punching bag, so heavy that if I tried to stand I would stagger, like those frail retirees that faint after standing on the queue for hours to collect their pension. The right and left sides of my head were at war with each other, they were battling for something, something that they both needed desperately, maybe they were fighting for blood.

Before I went to Benin to get my call-up letter I had visited my aunt in Enugu. Aunt Nkiru had given me the phone number of Chris, an uncle of ours who worked with the National Youth Service Corps, in case I encountered any problem with mobilization.

"Hello Uncle, it's me, Chibuzor, Nchedo's daughter. I just saw my posting letter – I was posted to Bauchi – Uncle please, how can you help me? I will never go to the north," I said in Igbo, my voice cracking.

"Why did you not tell me as soon as the list of the names of prospective corps members was released? Eh? Well, take it easy: you just have to report to camp."

"But is there no way out? I will not go to Bauchi for any reason."

"Chibuzor, do as I have told you. Get to the orientation camp in Bauchi first."

Later, Uncle Chris said there was nothing he could do. By this point, I had already cried a bucket full of tears, and my stubbornness and questions were beginning to irritate him.

"Now what do you want me to do? I have told you that no matter what, you just have to report to camp," he said, ending the call in annoyance. This only made me cry harder. *My God, what was I to do?*

While at the University of Benin where I had read philosophy, I was very studious and hardworking, and had graduated with a second class upper division. I prayed that I would be mobilized to any state in the South-South, or southwestern Nigeria. I just could not understand the news of my posting to Bauchi. *Why me?*

My phone rang; I answered "hello" in my croaky voice.

"It's me, Francis. Why are you sounding this way? Are you okay?"

"I was posted to Bauchi."

"Jesus!"

This was the worst part of it: whenever I told anyone I had been posted to Bauchi, they would begin exclaiming as if the world had come to an end. How did they expect me to feel? For goodness sake, I was not going to hell. I decided to start counseling myself before people gave a young girl like me high blood pressure.

"But don't worry", Francis continued on the phone, "there is a way out since you do not want to go: just bring N30,000 and everything will be resolved."

Although I was very happy to hear that, I did not have the money. After giving it a second thought, I felt that Francis was a very mischievous and crafty person, so I called another uncle of mine, who was a very good friend of his, to confirm how reliable Francis' information was.

"Hello Uncle Okechukwu, I was posted to Bauchi for the National Youth Service Corps."

"Chineke," he exclaimed.

"But the good news is that your friend Francis said he could help me with just N30, 000. He will influence it so that I will not go to Bauchi but will be reposted to any state of my choice and—"

"Don't even try it. Francis is the last person you can trust. Trust the devil, not Francis: he just duped his own mother." Uncle Okechuku said this before I could even finish speaking. At that point, it was clear to me that I had to stop crying and brace up. It was either I went to Bauchi or I forget about the national service. I called my dad and asked how far Bauchi was from Lagos. "My daughter, I will not lie to you; it is very far."

It was then about 11:30 pm; I had been crying since 4pm. I told my father that if I must travel to Bauchi then I must go by air. My dad became disturbed: as if the news of his only daughter being posted to Bauchi was not bad enough, there I was demanding for money to go by air.

"Hello, Daddy? I must go by air. I will not go by road or else I will not go to Bauchi. How can I sit in a bus for over twelve hours?"

I heard a female voice saying, "calm down, Chibuzor."

"Please, who is speaking?" I said in a very harsh voice. "Please give the phone to my dad."

"Please calm down. I am your fathers' colleague. I served in Bauchi and I enjoyed my service year; it was a wonderful experience for me. In fact, I gained weight before I came back."

"How often did you travel home?"

"I came home twice."

"How did you cope with the food?"

"You can get any food you want there, but the best part is it is very cheap; you know the cost of living in northern Nigeria is very cheap as compared to the south."

"Well, it is not as though food is the most important thing on my mind. Can you please tell me the ways I can be granted redeployment anywhere else, because there is no way that I will go to Bauchi."

"There are two ways you can be granted redeployment. The first is if you are truly married and you have a marriage certificate to prove it, then you will be posted to the state of your husband's residence. My dear, your father already told me that you are not married, but if you have a boyfriend you can tell him to marry you immediately so that you can be granted redeployment on marital grounds."

Was this person crazy? I could smell her sarcasm from miles away. She must be joking – how could she give me such a suggestion?

"No. Please, what is the other way?"

"The second way is to get an authentic medical report from a recognized hospital stating that you have a chronic health condition which means that you cannot be posted far from home as you have to be close to your family for sufficient care in case of any emergency. So do you have cancer, epilepsy, asthma–"

"God forbid, I do not have any chronic health disease," I immediately interrupted.

"Even if you have them, see, my sister, NYSC is one of the strongest institutions in Nigeria. They are aware of the dubious means corps members use to be redeployed to their states of preference. As such, they actually investigate to know if the person has an illness. Those that come to camp claiming they have such illnesses will be interrogated by camp officials and medical practitioners. Now, let us assume you pass that test: you cannot claim you have asthma, for instance, and fully engage in camp activities because you might not know who is watching you. My dear, NYSC is fun: it is a once-in-a–lifetime activity. Just go and catch your fun."

This lady failed to realize that for me, it was not always about *fun fun fun*; I was more concerned with ambition. What could I possibly achieve in a town I heard was bedeviled by illiteracy?

Then the lady continued.

"Go and serve there. Sometimes those things we hear about the north in the media are just rumors. My dear, I met really nice people there and I saved a lot from my allowance. Just go and I assure you, you will definitely tell another story. You will even visit Yankari National Park – I'm sure you know Yankari is in Bauchi. Oh! That place is a site to behold!"

"Hmmm – when did you serve?"

"I finished serving in 2009."

"Where were you posted to – I mean, your place of primary assignment?"

"I was posted to teach in a secondary school."

"In which local government did you serve?"

"Erm, erm... actually, it was my sister that served in Bauchi; I actually served in Taraba. Your father told us his only daughter had been posted to serve in Bauchi. But my sister is here."

"Bauchi is a lovely place to serve." Another voice was speaking on the phone. "I served in Bauchi."

"Please, who am I speaking with? Which of you served in Bauchi? Because no matter what you say, I will not serve in Bauchi." I did not allow her to say a word.

"Take it easy. I served in Ganjuwa Local Government Area and we camped in Wailo. You will enjoy your service year."

"But I just told you I would not go, I must redeploy."

"If you reject this posting you never can tell where you will be posted to next. I was first posted to Benue and I did not go – I did not even collect my call-up letter – and the next posting was Bauchi. Your application for relocation might not be approved and you will become frustrated until the service year comes to an end. My dear, just calm down," Chioma (that was her name) said to me. "Collect the letter and come to Lagos so that we can talk better."

I sighed. "Okay, thanks a lot for the encouragement."

I was still staying with Sophia in Benin. She was happy she had been posted to Delta. I had fallen out with her because of the funny comment she made about my posting: "I thought you said you left your posting in the hands of God. Why, then, are you this sad? Maybe it was God's will."

"How can you say this to me now? What you are saying is true, but is this the right way to say it, and is this the right time to say it?"

I did not know if she heard what I said because the continuous crying had cracked my voice. Even as I spoke to her, tears flowed down my cheeks. I went outside to remain under the mango tree in their compound. If she could not console me at this time when I needed her the most, then I would rather speak to my dad. Because of the falling-out I had with Sophia, I now appreciated my father's constant calls, his grand efforts to bring his only daughter out of her state of depression. *If he could show me this much love from a distance, how much further would he go when I finally got to Lagos?*

My phone was ringing again; I suspected it would be my mum. I was right.

"Hello Ada, your father just told me about your posting. Please wipe your tears; there will be a solution, *nne*, God will give us a solution to this problem. I can understand how you feel, I actually feel worse."

"Ok, ma." I went in to get another cup of water.

"Mirian, come." Sophia's mother held my hands and drew me into her room. "You are like a daughter to me – in fact, you are my daughter – please, keep calm. One thing I can assure you: this time will pass. Everything happens for a reason."

Sophia's mum's kind words were like ice drops on the walls of my grieved heart. She was there for me all the way, even though I was very paranoid. She probably knew as a mother that I was going through a lot psychologically and emotionally and I did not need any more worries to add to my existing issues. She counseled me and told me to take things easy as God was in control. I drew strength from what she said and it dawned on me that I had to stop being paranoid. I was not in my father's house and I was brought up by my mother to be a very disciplined and obedient child and to be very tolerant.

The next day I went to the university to collect my call-up letter. Ordinarily, Sophia and I would have gone together but because of my mood and the quarrel we had the night before, we left separately. I got to school and saw a massive crowd of graduates queuing to collect their letters. A course mate, upon sighting me, began sympathizing with me. Most of my friends had been posted to states in southern Nigeria; others who had been posted to states in the north were already looking for ways to redeploy. The most common way was to get a fake medical result. I called my mother to seek her opinion.

"Mummy, can't I just lie that I have an ulcer or asthma so that I can be redeployed?"

"Ada, in Jesus name you do not have those sicknesses. You are a child of God: don't even try it. You do not know what the future holds for you; what if it comes to pass? My daughter, you will regret this action if you carry it out. Just pray. The Lord is with you; your case will always be different, *nne biko qua*, I reject those sicknesses for you. As I speak to you I am on the mountain, I am standing in the gap."

Yes, pastor, I said in my mind. I had called the wrong person. It wasn't like I did not know what her response would be. Although she was not happy with my posting to Bauchi, she had no solution. You could never have a decent conversation with my mum without her talking or calling God. My mum prayed about everything; she believed she could do all things through Christ that strengthened her. This was the way she brought me up; she instilled this belief in me, but I still believed that *God for all, every man for himself*. I could never say this to her face, otherwise I would be asking for trouble; she would spend the whole day preaching and the next day asking for God to deliver me from the evil spirit, because to think that way was a clear manifestation of an evil spirit in the person.

I believe God has many children. Humans with all their evil deeds are very fond of their children – how much more God, who is all perfection and all Goodness? Yes, he said so in the Bible. I collected my call-up letter –

there it was, boldly written: my name, course of study, university, the state I was posted to, and the location of the NYSC camp in the state. The fantasy of a miracle happening was totally exterminated in my mind just like a flash. It was already getting late; I could not travel from Benin to Lagos so I had to spend the night at Sophia's house. Sophia's parents as always were very welcoming; she had a wonderful home. Her parents were so loving and caring. All through my days at the university, whenever I visited they took me in as their own daughter and gave me things and money. Their daughter Sophia and I had a lot in common: she was the only daughter among three brothers.

As she and I were not on talking terms, her mother continued to encourage and comfort me. I felt so much at home. The next morning I woke up and was set for the journey. Sophia's parents, who were civil servants, had already wished me a safe journey back home. I went to Sophia and told her I was going back. I did not understand why she was giving me attitude or maybe I was the one with the attitude; but she was supposed to understand and tolerate me, especially in my state of mind. I did not know who said what, but the next thing

I knew, we were yelling at each other. I was still speaking with tears in my eyes. I wondered why she did not feel my pain. Oh! My God, I miss home: my lovely brothers knew how to handle this part of me without causing me more pain. If they made any comment that made me flare up, they would immediately apologize and I would realize that there was no need to quarrel in the first place.

I left in annoyance. *Two wrongs do not make a right…Sophia should know that I am angry and not my normal self…she ought to be patient with me…she has every reason to be happy; she lives in Benin and was posted to Delta, I live in Lagos but was posted to Bauchi…as a good friend, she ought to be at my side to comfort me.* While we were quarreling, she said her mum told her to give me some space for a while because I had a lot going on in my mind and could be easily aggravated. I was heartbroken because I had not only quarreled with my closest friend, I had to also deal with the sad news of my posting to Bauchi.

I boarded a bus and headed for Lagos. Phone calls from people sympathizing over my posting to Bauchi made tears roll down my cheeks. My cousin Amaka called and told me that I could return the call-up letter and apply for the next batch. As I had left Benin and was very close to Lagos, I immediately called my friend Jerry to find out if I could return the letter. He said that there was a massive crowd of graduates from various faculties and that as a result, the staff would only attend to queries after everyone had collected their call-up letter. I had less than two days to report to the camp. If I did not go to Bauchi, the call-up letter might not be collected from me, and I would not know my fate regarding NYSC. On the other hand, if I went to Bauchi, I did not know if I would come back alive and I would not develop myself as I planned. Either way, I had something to lose. With all of these thoughts going through my mind, I got home safely and was happy to meet my family well.

PREPARATIONS FOR BAUCHI

Mr. and Mrs. Ayobami were the first people to welcome me when I returned to Lagos from Benin. They lived in the flat at the back of my compound. The love birds were on the veranda enjoying the breeze as usual.

"My black queen," Mr. Ayobami asked me, "why do you look so pale?" I was carrying my handbag so he did not know that I had travelled. I was used to him calling me pet names in front of his wife. They were a very young couple; even without a child after five years of marriage, the man still treasured his wife. So much more now she had gotten pregnant: he would wash her clothes, cook and perform other household chores when she was indisposed. The woman, for her part, respected her husband to a fault. *The most important thing to me is to have a wonderful family*, I thought, admiring this wonderful couple. Mrs. Ayobami rubbed my back from my neck to my waist. "Ebony girl why are your eyes so deep and red? Talk to us dear."

I immediately started crying. "I was posted to Bauchi for my NYSC."

"Congratulations baby! Is that why you are crying? My world, get her a chilled juice to calm her nerves so that we can celebrate her success," Mr. Ayobami said to his wife.

"Yes o!" Mrs. Ayobami answered.

"My dear so you are now a corps member. My younger brother, whom I spent all my money on to make sure he graduates from school, for ten years now..." Mr. Ayobami opened his eyes wide, and used his fingers to sign ten. "He is roaming about constituting a nuisance. Maybe he joined a cult. Well, that is his business. My dear, half loaf of bread is better than *puff puff*. You are very lucky: you graduated at the right time with a good result and you have been mobilized to serve your fatherland. God is the only security that is certain: just trust in him and Bauchi will not see your end."

"Amen o," his wife responded. She served me the hot *jollof* rice she had just prepared. Mrs. Ayobami was an excellent cook, and the aroma was out of this world. I finished the food while the couple told me comforting stories about why I should consider myself lucky to be called to serve my fatherland. Mr. Ayobami then left us to have a ladies talk.

"My dear, I know you will be wondering why my husband adores me. One of the reasons is that as a young girl I was very modest. I know you have always been a good girl. Please do not change when you go to camp and don't forget the family you are from. You are the first child and your younger ones look up to you."

I left their flat and went to mine to take a bath and rest. I knew that I would go to Bauchi. This lovely couple had no child yet they hardly quarreled; they were always happy. I drew strength from them and came to terms with reality that life is not always rosy.

My father returned from work and took me to Oyingbo and Chioma's house. I knew them but I had never spoken to them. They were the big girls on my street and I had thought they were snobs, and I was surprised to find that they were very approachable.

"Daddy's girl," the light-skinned lady shouted when she saw me. "So you are the one crying like a baby making your dad spend his money buying unnecessary airtime, eh? Take your time o." She reached out to me, grabbing my nose so that I could not breathe. I struggled to withdraw from her and regain my breath. She and her sister told me all the wonderful experiences they had serving in northern Nigeria. Chioma, who had served in Bauchi, told me that things were very cheap there. Listening to them speak, it was clear to me that I would make the journey to Bauchi, although another problem was how I was to sit in a bus for over twelve hours.

I rushed to braid my hair, and bought a few provisions and other necessary things I would need while in the camp. At the worst, I would simply apply for relocation while there. I woke up stronger the next morning. My dad went to Ijora to buy my ticket.

I had gone to IyaJide's shop to buy bread for breakfast when I saw Ayo's mother. I told her that I was posted to Bauchi; her son Ayo was currently serving in a northern state and had witnessed the post-election violence. I called him to find out if things had returned to normalcy.

"Ayo, it's me, Chibuzor, who lives on your street."

"Longest time, dear," Ayo replied.

"I was posted to Bauchi for NYSC–"

"What? I hope you are not considering going there for any reason."

"I am going to camp today," I replied.

"NYSC is not worth risking your life for. Are you not aware that Bauchi recorded the highest number of deaths of corps members during the post-election violence? Don't go, don't even think of it....well, it is your choice. Do whatever you want." He said this in a very harsh voice and ended the call. I immediately called my dad who had gone to book the bus ticket.

"Daddy, I just called Ayo, the son of the nurse who lives on our street. He asked me not to go. Please just forget about the ticket. Don't waste your money because I will not go."

"Hmm, okay," my dad answered me in a confused tone. My dad called my uncle who was at home to find out what I had just heard that made me change my mind.

"Chibuzor, your dad just called and said you are not going to Bauchi again, because of the telephone conversation you had with Ayo." Uncle Chinedu loved to preach; he must have been greatly influenced by my mother.

"You see, when you make up your mind to do something and you keep listening to what people are saying, you are likely to make a mistake. You have left your position in the hand of God, then let His will be done."

Whenever he spoke, he dragged his words, as if he did not know the next word to say. But I was touched by his sermon and I immediately called my dad.

"Okay Daddy, you can go back and get the ticket. I will go."

"I just alighted from that bus and I am presently in another going to work. But don't worry, I will get the ticket," my dad replied.

He called me later and told me to get ready for 12pm so that we could both go to the park. I met him at Mushin, and we took three extra city buses from Ikotun before we got to the park at Ijora.

JOURNEY TO BAUCHI

We got to the Ijora Park at 2:30. I was shocked by the massive crowd of people who wanted to travel to the north. A man with a cracked voice shouted, "*Oya*, come and show me your bag, make I put am for boot." All the travelers hurried in his direction and identified their luggage so that it could be loaded onto the bus. At 3:30 the bus driver was done with packing the luggage, and the bus left for Bauchi.

My father waited for me to board the bus. He had gotten me a ticket close to the window just as I liked. As soon as I sat down, I immediately tried to find him. Whenever I was travelling long distance he would always accompany me to the park: while I attended DDL Enugu, he would take me the park, just as he did when I gained admission to the University of Benin. He always waited for the bus to move before he would leave the park. He was not the type to tell you he loved you day and night, or tell you on Sundays that your dress looked good on you. I did not expect him to say this, but my mum did. She never heard it from his mouth, but I felt that if she listened deeply she would hear it from his heart, like I did. When the bus moved, we would keep waving at each other. I would keep stretching my neck to have one last glance of him, our eyes fixed on each other as though if either of us blinked the other would disappear, and he would keep following the bus until he couldn't see me anymore. He never knew that I cried after such long goodbyes; I never told him. Maybe he cried too. He would never admit it; he always told my younger brothers that a man never cries. My father's love for me was unquantifiable. He was proud of me, and our family friends and relatives would always tell me how he spoke grandly of me behind my back; he would never say any such thing to my face.

He wished me a safe journey and I thanked him for leaving his work appointments. His customers were calling him to hurry and come to the market, but he waited to be sure I was safe. He too was scared.

There were many young people in the same bus traveling to the north, the majority of who were also prospective corps members. There were only four of us posted to Bauchi, and the rest of them ganged up and were making jests at our expense, which made the other passengers laugh.

Less than thirty minutes after the bus left, Steve, a course mate of mine who was also posted to a state in northern Nigeria, called me. He was just like me: he too did not want to go to the north and had been looking for a way out. He spoke to me in a fast manner: "Mirian, as I speak to you, now look for a way to Abuja. Free redeployment is currently being granted to corps members posted to northern states and it ends today. As I speak to you I am in Abuja and I have been relocated. Just come and you will be relocated to any state other than your state of origin, and certainly not a northern state."

"Are you serious? Is this for real? I asked.

"Yes," he replied.

"Thanks for the information."

I immediately told the corps members in the bus about the development but they all started laughing at me. One of them said to me, "Do you think the federal government is stupid? How can they post corps members to the north with all the crises and still redeploy them?"

"*I tire o*!" one of the passenger replied in exclamation. The passengers debated the reliability of Steve's information.

Another course mate of mine, Brenda, who was also posted to Bornu, a state in northern Nigeria, called me and said she had stopped in Abuja and planned to continue the journey the next day because Bornu is very far from Delta, where she resided. She told me the same story as Steve.

"Mirian, I thought it was a joke but it is very real. In fact, they have collected my call-up number and are giving me a new number and call-up letter tomorrow."

"Why did you not tell me this earlier?" I asked her.

"I did not know. I just stopped at my aunty's place in Abuja and Noel called me to give me this information. Steve called me too, and I called you after I confirmed it." Her airtime ran out and the conversation ended. I had just paid N7000 to go to Bauchi: was I to stop the bus now and board a bus to Abuja? I was confused; I did not know what to do. I told the others in the bus and this time they believed that the information was true. Since I was going to the north, I thought that the driver would drive through Abuja so I called to the conductor, "Please, stop when you get to Abuja. I want to go to the NYSC headquarters at Maitama."

"My friend, we will pass Nasarawa, but Nasarawa is not far from Abuja. We will pass there between 12am and 1am." I told him to alert me when we got there. I was alert throughout the journey, constantly looking at my wristwatch. I was ready to take the boldest decision I would ever make so that I could return to the world of my dreams and have a fruitful service year. I woke up the other three corps members who had been posted to Bauchi and told them to get ready. I shouted to alert the conductor to stop the driver; it was 12am on the dot, the moment I had been waiting to salvage this depression I was feeling. I suddenly heard the voice of a lady. I turned around: it was the woman who had been reading a newspaper throughout the journey. She hadn't said a word, even when everyone was discussing our posting.

"Just look out of the window. You want to endanger your life by stopping in this thick forest in a strange land at this ungodly hour of the night? What risk can be worse than that? I would advise you to get to Bauchi: if no corps member was posted there and your posting was a mistake, then you can go back to Abuja. It is safer because it will be daylight. Please, your family is not here and I do not think they would support this idea."

Steve had called me again to find out my plan. I told him that I was told that the bus would pass through Nasarawa at midnight. He insisted that I alight there, but that I lodge in a hotel till daylight. I looked outside the window as the woman had asked me to, and it was indeed a thick forest: complete darkness everywhere. I could only see the tall trees because of the light from cars, and because it was midnight only a few cars were on the highway. I was scared, but I did not care; I felt that God had answered my prayers. That was why Steve and Brenda had called me.

While I was deep in thought Chinedu, one of the corps members posted to Bauchi, said to me in a sleepy voice.

"So if they leave you, you will come down at this time? How sure are you that they will answer you in Abuja? My dear, in this country it is about who you know. Let us go to Bauchi; we will all definitely redeploy. Besides, I have already calculated my transport; I do not have much for an extra journey."

I gave it a second thought and realized that if God really wanted me to redeploy, then Steve and Brenda would have called me before my dad paid for the ticket. I continued the journey but I was deeply disturbed.

The driver was fond of stopping at odd places to pick up passengers. There were no spare seats, and the new passengers – mostly men – would have to stand or inconvenience those seated by perching on the arms of the chairs and preventing you from resting your arms.

Everyone in bus began to panic at this behavior, especially the young corps members because we had never plied this route before and did not know what to expect. I now understood what people mean when they say that travelling at night was dangerous: it was not a mere child's play.

At 6:30 we arrived in Jos and more passengers boarded the bus. Bauchi is next to Plateau, so I looked out of the window to discover what the state was like. The town was calm: if it were Lagos, there would be traffic even at this early hour, but on the Jos road there were few buses on the road.

As we alighted from the luxurious bus, some men approached us. One of them had a small radio in his hands tuned to a station in Hausa, which I did not understand. The men could tell we were strangers from our mode of dressing, and they even knew where we were going to. I wondered how they knew, because I had been told that their level of education was minimal. They must have heard that it was that time of the year when corps members would be posted to different states from their radio. There were a lot of questions on my mind: some I figured out for myself, some left me at a loss. The people all dressed alike. Where I was coming from you would see different kinds of dressing, but in Bauchi everything seemed homogeneous.

We alighted at Gidan Mai and took a *keke napep* to Muda Lawal where we would take a bus to the orientation camp. When we got to Muda Lawal, I saw mostly men, tall and dressed in long caftans and caps complementary in color, which made them look even taller. I approached one and asked, "Please, what time will the bus leave for Wailo?"

"*Ba turenshi*, no English," he said to me, nodding his head in negation and flipping his fingers forward at me. Luckily, one person in our group had grown up in the north and was knowledgeable in Hausa. I could not wait for the bus to leave Muda Lawal. I was uncomfortable with the people and the surroundings.

While on our way to the orientation camp, Nnamdi, an architect from south-eastern Nigeria, said, "I have not seen a single two-storey building. My career is not here; I must redeploy." He kept complaining about it and we would all laugh. Bola, who had grown up in Bauchi, was very familiar with the surroundings. "Guys, stop laughing. When you are traveling to your villages, do you see any upstairs there? No, it is mostly huts and houses made of mud. It is the same with Bauchi. Come on, Bauchi is just a state like other states. I can bet you will enjoy serving in Bauchi. Just have an open mind. I know why you are all talking this way: it is because of the post-election violence. Bauchi is a peaceful place and everything has returned to normal. My friend, the architect, when you go to Bauchi town you will find storey buildings – some of them even built by your brothers from the east."

The others did not care to listen to Bola's sermon – they were cracking jokes and laughing – but I listened to everything she said and kept asking questions. We talked and laughed all the way until we got the orientation camp. The journey did not take as long as I thought it would because we all talked and lost track of time. I was sitting at the back and could not wait to alight from the bus to see what the camp looked like – or to hear that our posting to Bauchi was a mistake and that we would be reposted to other states.

Ouch! My head hit the door of the bus because of the way I jumped down. The floor was wet, and this made me slip. Nnamdi, who was tall and muscular, quickly grabbed me. *"Nne ndo* o! Sorry."

"Thanks, dear."

We said goodbye to the friendly driver who, even though we could not communicate because he did not speak English, made funny gestures. His son, who was with him, spoke in Hausa to Bola and told us not to be afraid. Bola translated his words into English and we were shocked at how a young boy could know that we were all scared. I told Bola to ask him how he could tell, and he responded that it was through our behavior.

I had had so many surprises: from Benin to Lagos, and now Bauchi.

ORIENTATION CAMP

After sitting in a bus for eighteen hours we finally arrived at 9:30am. I stretched my whole body and yawned endlessly. There were many soldiers and policemen at the NYSC Orientation camp, as well as civilians (presumably the NYSC officials); there was also a long queue of young people dressed in mufti. I asked one of them, "Please, what is the queue for?"

"You were posted to Bauchi, right?" he asked.

"Yes," I replied.

"So join the queue, it's for registration." So corps members had really been posted to Bauchi; I was not the only one, nor was it a mistake as I earlier hoped. We were many in number. The camp was a large expanse of land, with *dogonyaro* trees planted all over. The soldiers stood at strategic positions.

I joined the queue and was given the number 69, which was my batch number. I was also given a mattress and bed space. I was then to arrange my luggage, put on the NYSC uniform I was given to check how it fit and if it needed amendment, take a bath, rest, and get ready for business.

"I am hungry! Girls, let us go out to eat," Oge, my new friend shouted. I always had fat friends and they had one thing in common: food. My mum always warned me not to use the word "love" for inanimate objects. I knew she could not comprehend love of a different kind until she met my friend Oge. We all went out to eat at the *mami* market. I stopped chatting with the girls and descended on the hot plate of jollof rice I had just been served. The heat emanating from the food, accompanied with the aroma, made me sweat as I ate, so I also ordered a chilled drink.

"What are you doing there? Get up now! I'm talking to you girls. Get up!" I immediately put both pieces of meat in my mouth. A soldier had come up to us and asked us to quickly change and go to the parade ground where the rests of the corps members were. He couldn't be serious. He drew close to us and stretched out his cane to flog us, so we all ran. Oge, the fattest among us, was the first to get to the hostel. *Yes, he cannot enter the female hostel,* I said to myself. I was sweating and panting like someone who had just finished a marathon.

After few minutes, just when we thought we had escaped, I heard a loud feminine voice. "What are you girls doing there sitting and laughing? Do you think we are here to play? Change into your uniforms and run to the parade ground now!" I turned sluggishly to see a group of tall female soldiers. Their faces were definitely not friendly; one of them had a beard. I summoned the courage to speak to her politely.

"Please, I have sat down for eighteen hours from Lagos to Bauchi. I just arrived, and went to eat at the *mami* market. My joints are hurting me badly and–"

"Save those stories, my friend! And so what? Will you do what I asked you to do before I lose my temper?"

She started shaking the bunk beds with her other hand and with the ringing of the bells, the noise was too much, triggering the headaches I often experienced. I got up and changed into my NYSC uniform and headed for the parade ground. My friends, Oge and Ngozi, and I walked down slowly because we were tired from the long journey and weighed down by the food that we had just eaten. The hostel was not close to the parade ground, and as we struggled to walk a soldier shouted at us, "Double up, double up!" I did not know what he was saying. He looked at us and could tell that we were lost, then he shouted again, "If you are walking, then you are wrong!" I tried running but I was just too tired; so I tried jogging. As the saying goes: obey before complain. My friend Amaka bluntly said, "I can't run." One of fierce-looking soldiers told her to walk on her knees. She wanted to disobey, but when she turned and saw another fierce-looking soldier with his rod, she immediately complied with the punishment. I was happy I made the effort to jog; it was clear that they meant business.

After the rigorous training, I went to have a bath, tailored my uniform, and then went for a stroll with my friend.

In the evening I joined the Orientation Broadcasting Service, which was charged with the responsibility of disseminating information in the camp. I also met with the National Association of Catholic Corps members. I wanted to enjoy my time at the orientation camp because it was aonce-in-a-lifetime experience. I went to get dinner and slept like a baby.

At 5:00am the bugle was blown for everyone to assemble at the meditation ground. I ignored the signal: after all, NYSC officials were government workers – how could they wake up at 5:00am? But then I remembered the way my friend was punished and I quickly ran outside. Corps members who came late and walked leisurely were punished. We were first taught the NYSC anthem:

Youths obey the clarion call

Let us lift our nation high

Under the sun or in the rain

With dedication and selflessness

Nigeria is ours, Nigeria we serve.

After singing the NYSC and national anthems, we prayed both Christian and Muslim prayers, and the camp director, a plump woman of average height, came to address us.

"I congratulate you for successfully graduating from your various universities. I know most of you are already thinking you are corps members. Well, you are not corps members until you have been sworn in on Thursday 8th July, 2011. I implore you all to be disciplined: on Thursday after your induction, if you are found violating any of the NYSC by-laws the appropriate disciplinary action will be taken against you. Always queue according to your platoons."

After she spoke, the camp's public relations officer said,

"Corps members with the following numbers should wait."(In camp, you were not known by your name but by your number.)

"74 and 69, come out." One person came out, the other did not. He repeated,

"BA/11B/0069, come out."

I said to myself *,please whoever it is, go out so that we will not be punished*. Yesterday the camp and NYSC rules were read to us, which included that no one should be outside after 10 pm and we should all be properly kitted. I had not violated either rule, so I wasn't scared. He repeated the number again and it suddenly dawned on me that it was my number. I rushed out before he could call the number again. My heart was beating very fast. I asked myself what I could have done for my number to be called out on the meditation ground in the presence of all these people.

A man and a woman walked up to me and Emmanuel, number 74.

"Are you numbers 69 and 74?"

"Yes," we chorused together.

"I am the camp head of lectures and this man is my assistant. I am going to give both of you the task of summarizing all camp lectures."

We were given foolscap sheets to do the work. I wondered how she knew my number, then remembered that I had shown interest in the Orientation Broadcasting Service: that must have been where they got my number.

After the briefing we went to have breakfast, then headed straight to the lecture hall. In camp, you do not have time for yourself because the NYSC officials have planned everything for you.

Summarizing the lectures meant that I had to be attentive. At university, whenever a lecture was boring, I was tempted to sleep during lectures. I kept wondering how on earth I would stay awake every day for the three weeks the lectures would last.

We were all looking forward to the first lecture as the public relations officer announced that the director of the State Security Service would come to deliver a lecture on security. *So NYSC is aware that we want to leave and are doing anything to make us stay*, I thought to myself. *Let's hear what he would come to say.*

At 9am, a fleet of black cars arrived bearing the director of SSS and his entourage. He was a fair-skinned, handsome gentleman in his early 40s, and stood about 5 feet and 7 inches. He was dressed in a well-tailored and crisply ironed navy blue suit.

"This man is cute!" a female corps member exclaimed. Others did not say it openly, but we were definitely impressed with his looks.

"You are your own security. Listen to all the security tips I give you. You are free to ask as many questions as you like," he said as he began his lecture. I hoped some silly girls would not ask "Sir, what cream do you use?" or "What perfume are you wearing?" or "Who designed your dress?" Even though it sounded ridiculous, it was possible. Once when I was in secondary school our economics teacher, who was very strict, asked us to tell him one thing we liked about his teaching. One of my female classmates said, "I like the way you walk and please, can I know the name of perfume you are wearing? It has such a lovely fragrance." The whole class bursted into laughter, because the girl had been looking for a way to ask, but could not because the teacher was not approachable, and thought that now he was in a good mood, she could seize the opportunity.

The lecture hall was quiet; no one was speaking except for the director. All of the NYSC officials, including the camp director and state coordinator, were present. They were seated right in front of us. The soldiers and the platoon commanders sat with us the corps members so that we did not sleep or make distracting noises. Most of the corps members were writing or had their eyes on the director: even if they were not listening, he was worthy of beholding.

"Have two phones on separate networks, save distress messages as drafts, ensure you always have airtime on your different phones, do not always follow one route when going home or going to work. The federal government and the state have promised security to all the corps members posted to Bauchi. Save these phone numbers I will give you: ensure you call or send a message to us as soon as you sense danger."

The corps members saved the numbers called to be sure they were real phone numbers. The director was not only cute and charismatic, but also smart.

"Why are you all flashing the numbers? I told you to only save them, and to send text messages, flash or call when you sense danger. We used that number to rescue corps members in distress during the post-election violence. All the corps members that tried to reach us with these phone numbers were rescued."

I wondered how he knew that we were flashing the numbers because I did not hear a phone ring. At question time, the corps members who put their hands up were known clowns. As they came out with straight faces, we were all laughing because we knew they were not serious. I could not wait to hear their questions. The first corps member stepped up.

"Sir, you said that the government has promised security. I am sure of that, because I observed that the military men present here are more than the corps members. Will these military men be with us when we leave camp? Will they live with us in our houses and go with us to our places of primary assignment?"

The next corps member asked,

"When I checked my posting on the board I saw BA. I thought it was Bayelsa. When I realized it was Bauchi, I did not tell my parents. As I speak, my parents do not know I am in Bauchi. Since we are very few posted to Bauchi, please post all of us to Bauchi town for security reasons."

The corps members started clapping. The officials and the soldiers told us to stop. "When a corps member asks a question, let the director answer so he can get back to work. *Corpers we!*"

"Waa," we responded. The hall became quiet for the next question. A very tall female corps member with a straight face asked her question.

"You have been telling us about having two phones and not always taking one route. What if one is caught unawares? Like you opened your door and were attacked? What will we do? Please, we need to be taught self-defense skills like martial arts, so that when the need arises we know what to do. I am asking these questions because I do not want to redeploy o, I want to stay o." Before she finished asking her question, the lecture hall became rowdy as everyone was applauding.

The director smiled. He was not surprised at the questions the corps members were asking. Everyone was indeed afraid. I thought someone might jokingly admire the director, but they all went straight to the point. My eyes were fixed on the director as if I had been asked to also jot down the expression on his face. The PRO asked us to keep quiet and handed over the microphone to the director. He took a deep breath before he answered the questions.

"To the young lady who asked to be taught martial art for self-defense: I admire your courage, but please do not think of attacking people who are armed with guns or cutlasses with just your bare hands. Ensure you are always alert and you are always with your phone, No one will hurt you. What happened then, which you all are scared of, was post-election violence. As for the second question: we used to have over 1000 corps members posted to Bauchi but you are fewer than 500 now. This is so that we can closely monitor you, so please be calm and rest assured that all of you will be posted to Bauchi town where you can be easily reached. To the first question, like I said you are your own security. Just be alert and report any suspicious act. Bauchi is a peaceful state and I can assure you that your security is guaranteed."

A corps member was called to give a vote of thanks. There were mixed feelings: some were happy that all corps members would serve in Bauchi town, others felt like the questions were not fully answered. My father kept calling to find how exactly I was doing. His mind was not at rest.

The next lecture was about Bauchi and its culture. I wondered if the choice of topics of the first two lectures was deliberate. The state coordinator, who was introduced by the public relations officer, took up the microphone to address us.

"Corpers we!"

"Wa!"

"Corpers we we weo!"

"Wa wa wa o!"

"Once again, you are welcome to Bauchi State, the pearl of culture and tourism. I know that you will enjoy your service year in Bauchi. I want to give you a brief rundown of the history of NYSC, which I know some of you already have knowledge of. This scheme was established to reorganize the country after the Civil War. The unfortunate antecedents in our national history gave impetus to the establishment of the National Youth Service Corps by decree No 24 of 22nd May, 1973 under the leadership of General Yabubu Gowon, with a view to the encouragement and development of common ties among the youths of Nigeria and the promotion of national unity.

"There are four cardinal points upon which the scheme is based: the orientation course, primary assignment, community development services and passing out. Graduates below the age of thirty, like you all seated here, are qualified to take part in this year of mandatory service.

"The orientation course is a three-week training programme to prepare corps members for the year national service, as well as give room for you to interact amongst yourselves.

"At the end of the orientation exercise, you will be posted to your place of primary assignment to provide assistance to your various institutions. In addition, you will take up various projects individually or collectively to the betterment of your host community." He paused.

"*Corpers we!*"

"*Wa!*"

The tall state coordinator wore a long caftan and cap. A man in his late fifties, he was a good storyteller. As he addressed us he walked from one pillar to the next, maintaining eye contact to ensure that none of us were sleeping. I was seated at the front and my eyes met with his eyes several times; so much so that I began to wonder if his lecture notes were on my face.

He cleared his throat and continued.

"To come last is the passing out ceremony, at which the curtains will be drawn and I expect you all to bow down honorably to the clarion call. Do not abscond from service as disciplinary measures will be taken up against such. Be on your best behavior."

We all applauded him for his informative lecture. He then gave the microphone to the Hausa lecturer who would guide us through the introductory aspects of the Hausa language.

"*Inakwana* means 'good morning'; Ina*wuni* and *inagajiya* mean 'good afternoon' and 'good evening,' he began. He had a tiny voice, and I could barely differentiate between the English translations and the Hausa phrases. The responsibility I had been given made me very attentive: if I had not been given that task, I am quite sure I would have rested my back on my chair and slept during the lectures, using my notebook to block my face like those seated at the back were doing. Now I had no choice but to listen, but I was glad because I was unconsciously memorizing all of the camp lectures.

The Hausa lecturer continued, "But you can also say *sanu* to greet one person and *sanun ku* to two people or more." He asked us to repeat after him. Some of the corps members mischievously repeated "*sanu ukwu*" ("*ukwu* "means a woman's waist or hip in Igbo language.) He continued, "*Daya* is one, *biyu* is two, *ukwu* is three…" *Ukwu again*, I said to myself. These boys would have a lot to laugh about. The Hausa lecturer did not know why we were laughing as he did not speak Igbo.

After the lectures for the day ended, the camp director asked us to wash our NYSC ceremonial wear and prepare for our induction on Thursday as top dignitaries from the government and military would be in attendance.

The camp commandant, a soldier, also spoke to us. He told us to assemble at the parade at "1500 hours" for parade rehearsals. "Ha!" we shouted, because we were exhausted after sitting for so long, After queuing for lunch washing our ceremonial wear, there would be no time to rest.

"Keep quiet!" the camp commandant shouted, pointing at us.

"You should all learn to multitask: as you are easing yourself in the toilet you can also wash." It sounded so strange that we started laughing.

"What is funny? Stop laughing or I will not release you to have lunch, and you will stay here till 1900 hours!"

"Ah! Sorry sir," we pleaded.

"Sit up!" he commanded. "Now you can stand up row by row – no rushing, do you hear me?"

"Yes sir."

We all went to have lunch, cleaned up and headed straight to the parade ground; as usual, latecomers were punished.

PASSING OUT OF ORIENTATION CAMP

At 7am on the day of our induction, all of the corps members were already on the parade ground. The whole camp was tidied – not a single empty water sachet or biscuit wrapper could be seen. We were a sight to behold, neatly dressed in our caps, NYSC crested vests, khaki trousers, socks and jungle boots. The band was on one side of the field.

"Now you have one last chance to get it right before the dignitaries arrive, said our camp commandant. "I want no mistakes – if you know you have a life-threatening illness, leave now." His voice was aggressive, and he opened his eyes wide as he spoke.

"I want no *banza banza*; now, get it together – don't disgrace me, don't spoil my parade o! Do you understand?" He stressed the last three words.

"Yes, sir!"

"The parade commander was a woman. She was strong and had a loud masculine voice: when she shouted, the whole parade heard her. In NYSC, there were no *women*: we were all addressed as *gentlemen corps members*. She shouted, *"Parade shun,"* stressing the second syllable of the first word. I could feel the thunder of her words; she shouted not only with the strength in her voice, but with energy from her stomach. She continued, "Parade will form two lines from three lines. Look to your left and take dressing; look to your   right and take dressing!"

With swift, organized movements, the corps members moved into position and the band began beating their drums. After two days of rigorous training, we had mastered the parade so well that we could pass for professional soldiers. It was a bright day and the sun was punishing hot, hot enough to bake a loaf of bread.

I had been appointed the vice president of the OBS. Although I had participated in parade rehearsals, I had not yet been released from my duties to join in the march past. Some of the corps members who were in the parade were looking for an excuse not to march; I could not understand why they did not want to take part in this once-a-lifetime opportunity. As I watched from a distance, I was awed by their order. The soldiers manned their platoons; the parade commander, quarter guards, sub guards – all of them were on point. "I must join them," I said to myself. The rest of the OBS crew and I had already put the necessary logistics in place, so I boldly ran to the field to join them, but the NYSC official who assisted us shouted at me, "Will you come back here?"

"But sir, all the logistics are in place, and I participated in the rehearsals. Please let me join them," I pleaded.

"You are not serious; you are the next in command. Look, if anyone is to join them to march, it should not be you. Who told you that you are done? You will also have a lot of work to do when the guests arrive." He sighed. "I don't understand you, this girl. They are all standing in the sun looking for excuses not to parade, and you who have the luxury of sitting in the shade want to go and join them."

"Go now," Chinedu the OBS president added sarcastically.

I did not want to be like those who did not want to march and came up with various excuses to avoid it, whether OBS, fake pregnancies, or sickness. I wanted to enjoy camp and gain as many wonderful experiences as I could, so that I would not later regret not doing anything.

All the guests arrived and the parade began. The parade commander did very well and the parade was perfect; all of the corps members moved in harmony. I wished I was parading with them: their heads up, their legs moving up and down in sync, their arms like sharp currents in a deep sea, their shoulders high, and their chests out. They paraded passionately with all their heart and strength as the national anthem played. These promising young people were like soldiers going to war with their country's victory as their priority. I thought that even if they got no job after NYSC, if they put this same passion into a trade, they would be unstoppable.

I was, as always, so carried away by my thoughts that I did not realize when the parade ended. A journalist sought the permission of the state coordinator to interview us (as it was against the NYSC by-laws for a corps member to speak to the press without authorization).

Camp was becoming interesting. The rate at which I cried each day about Bauchi drastically reduced: maybe because I had cried so much that my eyes could not secrete more tears, or because I was having a good time, as much as I did not want to admit it. I made friends and became popular in the camp. Because I always wore the OBS badge I was called "OBS," but of course I was not as popular as the president of OBS, Chinedu, who was a funny person.

We were soon asked to get ready for the various inter-platoon competitions in dance, drama, sport, cooking and beauty. I joined my platoon for the dance and drama rehearsals. I was knocked out of the girls' volleyball early; I was never good at sports, so I knew I was not going to be chosen.

People were bonding fast at the camp. Some of them were falling in love – some even started dating right there in camp, sensing a promising future. The couples always seen together were teased by the state coordinator, who told them that there was a charge levied for corps members that met and got married in camp.

The Millennium Development Goals (MDG's) group gave us a lecture and asked that those who were interested in their training to join them. I enjoyed their lecture and decided to join the training. I was about to rush off to the *mami* market during a break when a voice called me: "Hello – please, excuse me. My name is Felix – your face looks familiar. Do you live in Port Harcourt?" I turned round to see a young man of average height.

"Nope, I don't live in PH."

"Have you ever been to Port Harcourt?"

"Nope."

"I will remember where I have previously seen you."

"Ok then. See you later – let me quickly get a drink before the break is over."

"Alright, it was really nice meeting you."

During the MDG's volunteer training, he kept staring at me. At that point, I figured out that he had never seen me and was only looking for an opportunity to talk to me. These guys and their toasting techniques! Ezuma was another one. He was a serious-minded academician, a good motivator and very resourceful. He had impeccable grammar – it was no wonder he played the role of the professor in our platoon's drama. He was the kind of guy you would never believe could woo a woman. I enjoyed his company – he could lift your spirit effortlessly. He was knowledgeable on many topics and as a result, we bonded fast.

The next morning was the day of the endurance trek. We knew to prepare for the long walk the previous day. Its aim was to give the corps members stamina and instill a spirit of perseverance.

"Good morning, gentlemen corps members," the camp director said.

"Good morning, ma," we responded.

"I can see you all are ready for the long walk – please, stay in line."

The next thing I heard was our platoon commander chanting, *"Echebe, Echebe, Moral high!"* We all joined the chanting, with our boots hitting the ground. As we jogged with the soldiers leading us, the environment was charged and the ground vibrated I was surprised to see corps members who had dodged the march past and other strenuous camp activities join the platoon for this memorable exercise. As we jogged, the songs continued:

"See how dey dey look o, see how dem dey look o, lazy people!"

I felt like a patriot, ready to give up my life for my country. Yes, I was a patriot: I came all the way from home to the distant north, a place where I knew no one and had never been. If not for NYSC, would I have ever gone to the north? I mingled and became friends with total strangers. I wish we wouldn't stop.

Thirty minutes passed and we had yet not gotten to our destination. My legs were beginning to ache and I was short of breath. It was not fun anymore, and I wanted to stop and rest for a while.

"If you are walking, you are wrong!" I was surprised that this soldier knew what was on my mind. "Double up, double up," he commanded in a harsher tone.

I sighted hills in the distance as we jogged on. *It must be a mirage – when we get closer the ground will be level*, I said to myself. But as we approached, it did not level – they were real! We would have to climb the rocky hills to continue.

I was tired and asked Ezuma, "When will I stop getting surprises? How can they expect us to climb these hills?"

"Mirian, did you believe that you could climb the rope and even walk on those tiny rods during yesterday's Man-O-War training? But you made an attempt, right? And you succeeded! Why not make an attempt now, too?"

Ezuma the motivational speaker placed my hands on his shoulders to help me lift my weight as we climbed the hills. And then he said something that I suspected had been on his mind for a while.

"If we are not granted redeployment then let us stay. Let us not push the redeploying further like the rest. No! – We will make it happen here in Bauchi. Mirian, we will leave our footprints on the sand of time. Bauchi will never forget us," my friend said emphatically. I was too tired to respond.

Soon we were on the other side of the hills. Although I was still in my country, I felt like I was in a strange land, like a tourist. Everything was so different. We were in a small settlement with houses made of mud, and stopped to buy water to quench our thirst. The children in the village were so excited to see us. Although they could not speak English and we could not speak Hausa, we somehow understood each other. The young girls fascinated me – their hands and legs were beautifully decorated with what seemed like tattoos but in artistic floral designs. The littlest girls- aged two or so - were dressed like their mothers: their entire bodies covered, revealing only their face, hands and feet. The older girls – aged seven or so – wore local make-up to enhance their eyes and lips. My mother never allowed me wear make-up at that age, but these kids were adorable. Their smiles were so generous; they made you want to give them all you had in your pocket. They looked so innocent. I did not know if someone told them we were coming, because to me it seemed as though they had anticipated our arrival. They played drums for us to dance to, and they danced along with us.

It was then time for us to go back. Most of the kids accompanied us halfway. The village gave me an idea of what life must have been like in pre-colonial times.

We got back to the camp exhausted. I went to have lunch and then continued dance and drama rehearsals. I was the narrator of my platoon's drama and one of the lead dancers. My platoon was excited to come first and second respectively in the competitions: we did not believe we would perform well as we had quarreled a lot during the rehearsals. Afterwards, my name was taken down by a corps member. When I asked why, he said that the camp head of socials had asked him to do so. I looked at his list and asked him why everyone who participated in the competition was not on it, but he just smiled.

We had finished all the sports and cultural competitions and the orientation camp was gradually coming to an end. I was beginning to like the lovely people I had met there, especially Aisha and Zainab who never stopped telling me about *fura de nunu*, their favorite local dairy product. But nostalgia for my life before set in once in a while.

I applied for relocation like many others. We did not have any strong basis for applying: we just did to follow the bandwagon because if everyone else was relocated, we did not want to be left behind. I was still uncertain, but some, like Nnamdi, my architect friend, wanted to be redeployed at all costs.

The night before the orientation closing ceremony, the list of those who had been redeployed on health and marital grounds was pasted. I ran to the notice board along with everyone – including the sick and expectant mothers – after parade rehearsals. My heart was beating fast.

"Your name is Mirian, right?"

"Yes," I answered.

"I saw your name – congrats, you have been redeployed."

"What!" I exclaimed. *Congratulations?* I did not know if I was happy or sad – was it good or bad news? The girl who told me the news looked at me strangely and walked away. I stood for a while thinking, and then went to the notice board to see for myself.

There were many corps members, so I squeezed myself into the crowd and managed to get a space from which I was able to view the list. I checked it over and over again. *Oh, she must have thought Mirian Ude was my name.* I smiled. When I got to the hostel, most of the girls were crying because they were not redeployed.

"Mirian, you are not crying, that you were not redeployed?" Ngozi asked.

"My dear, I have to be happy. I am neither dead nor sick; I really want to see what the future holds for me. Maybe it is my destiny."

The next morning those who were redeployed like Nnamdi and my other friends collected their letters, packed their belongings and left for their various states, while those who were not reposted headed to the parade ground for the closing ceremony. There were few people in the parade because many of those who were redeployed had been in key roles. The camp commandant was angry at this development, as he did not want the dignitaries to think that we had not been properly taught how to parade. Those of us in the OBS crew that did not parade during the opening ceremony had to join in. I smiled as if I had won a lottery, and my friends asked again why I was always happy doing what other people would not be happy with. I answered, "I parade well. A lizard that climbs down from a tall tree and nobody praises would nod its head."

After the parade we went to the lecture hall to collect our posting letters. I was eager to collect mine, but it was a long queue which some people were not patient enough to join. This caused quarrels among the corps members. I finally collected my letter and discovered that I had been posted to the Bauchi State Television Authority (BATV) as my Primary Place of Assignment (PPA) I was excited because I loved broadcasting. I boarded a bus from the National Association of Catholic Corps Members which conveyed us to town. I had lunch and took a motorcycle to Wuntin Dada where BATV is located, but was told to come back the next day so that I would be accepted. I had been told earlier to report to my PPA the following day, but I was curious to see what the place looked like.

The next morning we all woke at 5am, prayed together and attended mass. After helping out with the household chores I said to myself, *this is another Wailo camp*. I had breakfast and headed to my PPA. Everyone was very friendly and I was accepted that same day. I then reported to the NYSC secretariat to continue the registration process.

I applied for casual leave to enable me to travel home and come back fully prepared. After two days, I left Bauchi for Lagos. It was another night journey, but I had no choice: if I went by air, I would exhaust my monthly allowance; if I took a morning bus, I would arrive in Lagos late at night. The bus passengers included other corps members, who made the journey lively. When we arrived in Lagos, I didn't need the conductor to wake me up, between the traffic and the bus conductors shouting "*Oshodi, oshodi*". I looked forward to seeing my family and the Ayobamis.

I opened the gate and struggled in with my belongings. Our gate was in bad shape: the metal was rusted and it couldn't be locked at night. Perhaps the landlords were waiting for the compound to be robbed before fixing it. My younger brothers had been monitoring the gate, and immediately rushed to help me out with my luggage. I hugged them excitedly, then looked around. The compound was dirty; everywhere was quiet. "Where are our neighbors, the Ayobamis?" I asked one of my younger brothers.

"I have not seen them for a week now."

"Is there any problem? Where did they go? Are they alright?"

"I don't know," he answered.

I was worried and wanted to know where they were. I could not wait for my dad to come back. Even though I was happy to have arrived home safely, something was missing, my joy was not complete — not just because of the delicious dish Mrs. Ayobami would have served me, but because of the way I would have been welcomed if they had been in. They could make a depressed person feel loved with their unconditional showering of affection.

In the evening my dad returned from a long and stressful day at work. We were happy to see each other; my father would usually not talk to anyone when he was that tired, but he kept asking me questions. After some time I boldly asked him: "Daddy, what of our neighbors, Mr. and Mrs. Ayobami? I have not seen them since I came back. Have you spoken to them?" My dad could be very sarcastic, sometimes answering question with questions.

"Call them *nah*, are they not your friends*?*" he said.

"When I got back I called their line but it was switched off."

"*Ehehnn, so?*" my dad asked.

Suddenly we heard noises and my dad asked me to check what it was. My brothers were good at fighting, so I thought it would be them.

"What is wrong with you, Kc and Nedu?" I shouted. But my brothers were not together, so the noise could not have come from them. I asked them if they heard the noise and where they thought it came from. Kc said it was from outside. I looked out of the window and noticed movement in the Ayobamis' flat. I rushed over and saw the couple with a group of relatives and we hugged each other. Mrs. Ayobami's mother-in-law shouted, "Please, take it easy!" I wondered why, as she had seen us hug that way many times. Mrs. Ayobami looked very great; her face was shining like never before. Her husband wore a very big smile, as were their relatives. This was unusual as normally when their in-laws came around, the couple would be troubled because of their child problem. Often they would come to our flat to escape from family pressure.

The suspense was becoming too much. "What is going on?" I asked. Just then I heard the cry of a baby and then it all added up.

"My God!" I exclaimed. "Jesus!" The baby was passed over to me and I saw the striking resemblance between the baby and the father. The baby was gorgeous; I could not contain my joy. "Congratulations! I am so happy for you. You will have more cute babies." Everyone chorused, "Alleluia!"

Children are the blessing of every marriage, I thought to myself.

"Mrs. Ayobami, I was so worried. I even tried your phone but it wasn't going through."

"We were at the hospital. The delivery was complicated, but thank God, it was a success. We continued chatting until her mother-in-law asked me to allow her to rest; I rushed home to give the good news to my parents.

That night I slept better than I had in a while.

The next morning I went to visit my friends. Everyone on my street gave me second looks, which was not strange: they could be very nosy. When I was still at university and came home for holidays, after some time they would start asking me when I would go back to school. So as usual they asked, "It has been long since we last saw you. Where did you go?"

"I went for service," I answered.

"Where were you posted to?" The question was inevitable. I told them I was posted to the north, and as expected they exclaimed and shouted. As I approached our street junction I knew more questions would be asked, so I waved greetings and pretended as though my phone was ringing so that I could walk on freely. I was, however, gradually becoming immune to people's reaction about where I was serving.

I went to visit my cousin, Amaka, at her husband's house in FESTAC. We were happy to see each other. Her husband was not comfortable with my posting and contacted his friend to help out with my redeployment. I had made up my mind not to redeploy, but after listening to him I changed my mind again. When my dad came home in the evening I immediately told him the good news about Amaka's husband helping out with my reposting. He was optimistic it would work out.

The Ayobamis made me laugh as usual when I told them about Amaka's husband helping me to redeploy. They advised that I be happy because I had every reason to be.

The two weeks granted to me was soon over, and it was time to head back to Bauchi for the service year proper.

THE EXPLOSION

I arrived back to Bauchi safely, and was welcomed by the catholic corps members at the lodge we shared. The next day was a day off for me at my PPA so I just stayed indoors to do some reading and have enough rest. I was relieved that I would not suffer the harsh sun. The NYSC morale and passion had dropped. Back at home I would stand before the mirror and mimic broadcasters. I used to daydream that one day my sonorous voice would be on air waves. It was surprising that now when I had the opportunity I was no longer as interested. I wanted to make a request for transfer to the admin department, so that I would only have to go to the office once a week.

At about 1pm most of the corps members were returning back form their various places of assignments. Felix, Chinedu and Steve came back together, their voices as they argued intruded into my long period of reflection.

"Is anybody here?" Chinedu shouted.

"*Mehn* I am so damn hungry" said Felix, whose mouth was always busy eating something and yet his body never was proof that he could swallow a cow. I came out of my room to greet them. "Hey guys, how was work? Hope you all are enjoying your various places of primary assignment?"

"Mirian! Mirian! Mirian! How many times did l call you?" Please, spare me your sarcasm; this is not time for it." I was taken aback. Steve was in a sort of bad mood, it was obvious from his outburst.

"How can we be enjoying the work here," he continued. "l still do not understand why this part of the country is being ravaged by poverty. In the school where I was posted there are no chairs. All the pupils sit on the bare ground."

I wanted to ask him if there were no such schools in the interior parts of his home state but I immediately remembered he just warned me not to be sarcastic. Besides it wasn't a valid argument. I also knew he stammered and my dear mother said I should be careful with people like that because when their speech is impeded they are quick to use their hands as solace. Chinedu now spoke, "As much as I don't want to remain here in the north. I feel compassion for the people living here. The teachers from the southern part of the country have all gone. The place is going backwards. You know a place becomes civilized and developed from the ideas and innovations that come in from the outside. But nobody wants to come here anymore. Everyone is leaving the north. My uncle, a merchant, who was born and bred in Maidugiri, had to leave the north in a hurry. He returned to his hometown with nothing. He had several houses and businesses in Maiduguri but they were all lost. When will all these end? I can't wait to leave here o," he finished.

A somber mood descended on all of us.

More corps members returned from work and the mood triggered more conversation on the subject of the instability in northern Nigeria.

"I was born and bred in the north," said Steve, taking a chair. "I speak Hausa more than Igbo which is my mother tongue. This north was a land flowing with milk and honey. *Haba* who will not love to visit Yankari

Game Reserve or to travel to buy quality but cheap gold from the city of Kano -a city that is hundreds of years old. When we were growing up, there was security. Our house didn't need fence or a gate. People could travel and leave their homes unlocked and nothing will go missing. The northerners and southerners ate in each other's homes. Don't we all remember when white people loved to stay in Jos because of its perfect weather? *Kai*, it is painful o, especially for those of us who knew how things were." He paused and looked around at everyone. "What do you think we can do as youths of this country? What can we do?" It wasn't clear if it was a question of defeat and resignation or if he actually wanted answers. At any rate, no one had an answer. I wanted to speak but I was scared. It did not seem like I was in the company of my fellow corps members. The tension was palpable. Felix with a newspaper in hand as always, sighed heavily. Felix was known to have different perspective on things and was often seen as controversial.

"I know you guys will say I have come again, but before you tackle any issue you must look back into its history. Now when did all these start? Yes, I remember when I saw on Aljazeera the bodies of Boko Haram members who were killed. The in-law of the leader who went to enquire about the death of their leader was killed too, extra judiciously. Did anyone see the injustice? Look, they may have gone too far but they believed that they were fighting a just cause. Why is it that their violence is now deemed as terrorism? What about the militants in the south-south. Are they also not violent? But they were given amnesty? The solution is showing compassion to the deprived part of the country, they need help, simple!

"My friend will you shut that hole you call mouth? We have more northerners occupying political positions in the country, so whose fault is it that they do not help their people. Do you realize that the harsh consequences of their activities, like massive departure from the region will not only constitute a depletion of economic affairs in the north as happened in Basque country of Spain, but will throw those who are departing from the north into financial and psychological pressures. Nigeria has a population of 170 million our failure will mean hard ship for millions within sub Saharan Africa. What are you telling me sef?" Chinedu said with disgust.

"It is this 'their people', 'our people' that is causing all these problems. Are we not a country? Why are we waiting for 'their people' to help 'their people' when we are all of the same country? We are in it together. So Chinedu stop bringing tribal sentiments into the matter. We all have taken the bold step to come to the north to serve our father land; we have seen things for ourselves with our own eyes. I am not supporting Boko-Haram but do you think that the northerners are happy with what is happening? No!" Felix said with his small eyes widely opened to emphasize his point. "They are losing a lot. We are all losing. We need help." Felix was used to arguing calmly but now his mannerisms where becoming similar to that of Steve and Chinedu.

All the while they argued I was so carried away that I did not grab a chair to sit as others did, or maybe because I was not as tired as they were. I stood at the rear and listened to every one bare their minds. Wherever two or more Nigerians gather to discuss passionately, it was either about football or the state of the nation.

I wish there would be less passionate talk and more passionate doings. I wish we had good roads, and constant supply of electricity, I wish I could solve all these problems and put smiles on the faces of innocent, patient and hopeful Nigerians. We need our leaders, now, more than ever. We need good, compassionate leaders. I resolved that it would not be enough to just argue, but I must do something, no matter how small. I had not wanted to be here in Bauchi, but Nigeria is my country and I will go wherever I needed to go to serve my country.

Later that Afternoon, I got a call from the NYSC Secretariat. "Hello, is this Chibuzor Mirian Azubuike, BA/11B/0069? Report to the NYSC Secretariat; the state coordinator wants to see you."

"Any problem?"

"Just do what I have asked you to do," the male voice answered in a harsh voice.

What could the problem be? I asked myself. *Why would he want to see me?*

I asked the other corps members if they had gotten a call from the state coordinator: they all said no. I changed into my NYSC outfit and headed to the secretariat. I got there and asked for Mr. Alex as I had been told to do. I was directed to his office. The man seated behind the desk told me that I had been selected by the state coordinator to represent Bauchi in the north-east regional phase of the Director General's sport and cultural competition. I was shocked and wondered how they got my name – oh! I remembered that in camp, after our platoon dance and drama performances, my name had been written down by a corps member who refused to tell me what his list was meant for. The names of all who had performed well had been taken down. We would begin rehearsals the next day at the multipurpose hall.

I went to work in the morning and to rehearsals in the evening. It was very stressful, and we were later given letters to present to our employers to give us a few days off for training and the competition itself. I took the letter as instructed to the office of the managing director and handed the letter over to him to read.

"Wait, you are a corps member? I did not know that a corps member was posted here. What department were you posted to?"

"Admin."

"Who posted you to admin? You have no business there." He was beginning to raise his voice. "You ought to be in the department of news and current affairs. You have a great voice: I believe it will sound good on air. And you also have good diction. You shouldn't be in that department, unless you just want to waste away – but I won't allow that to happen. Go and call me Mr. Kepas."

I rushed to call him.

"Why did you post her to admin?" the managing director asked Mr. Kepas. He looked at me; we were both speechless.

"Mr. Kepas had posted me to the news department earlier; I went to meet him soon after to ask him to re-post me to admin."

I wondered why I had made this decision: the news was something I had a passion for and there was work to do there, while in the admin there was nothing – I didn't even have to be at the office every day. I had put Mr. Kepas in *wahala*; I hoped he would not lose his job because of me as we never told the managing director of the change.

"Now, go for your competition; when you come back, you will return to the news and current affairs department."

I left the office, but Mr. Kepas remained. I waited for him outside to be sure that I did not make him lose his job. After few minutes he came out, a frown on his face. "*Haba corper*, you just put me for *wahala*. I just pity you because you *dey fear fear*, but don't worry, nothing will happen to you here. The MD is right: you will learn a lot in the news department."

"*Nagode*, sir."

"*Toh, sai anjima*, good luck with your competition."

We traveled to Jigawa for the competition. I introduced the dance and played multiple roles in the drama. Our instructors were good and we were optimistic we would come first in one or both. But when the results were called, we came second in drama and fourth in dance. We felt bad – some people were even crying – but we knew we had tried our best. We supported the Bauchi boys in the football and they came first. That put smiles on our faces.

I resumed work in the news and current affairs department. The MD and some of the Directors encouraged me. Serving with BATV made me realize that broadcasting should be my profession, even though I had no degree in that subject area.

I was attached to several reporters to learn how their work was done. My first report was a project I initiated during our weekly meetings. I went to the office of the Bauchi NYSC state coordinator to find out their level of preparedness for the Batch C orientation camp. I submitted my report to Anti Fibi, the editor on duty. She was a very critical editor but always spoke calmly. She read and edited it, then I went to the studio and read it. The next day I got many compliments on my work. I once read in a book that when people tell you that you are talented in a particular field, you should consider taking it up seriously because they have discovered something you may not have. I concentrated on learning more and took the job seriously, learning the dos and don'ts.

One day, a few of us went on an assignment to a village called Bigi Tudunwada in the Bauchi LGA. A population of over 6000 drank from only one well and as a result often suffered from bad health conditions. I immediately made up my mind to do something. I wrote to the NYSC secretariat seeking permission to take this up as a community development project. I also sewed uniforms for pupils who had none.

Months passed and it was time for Christmas. I wrote for approval and traveled home to see my family. I ate and drank and added some weight. When the holiday was over, there was pressure on me not to go back to Bauchi. This was because Boko-Haram had threatened all the southerners in the north. Northerners in the south, especially those in Onitsha, were also leaving. Everyone was calling me, asking me not to travel again. My parents were scared. But I took my luggage and headed to Bauchi. Most of the corps members had not returned; the few who were around did not travel during the holiday. When my relatives called and I told them I had traveled back, they asked why I did not value my life. They were angry because not only did I travel back, but I was also living adjacent to a church which was a target.

Amaka's husband asked why I didn't at least pity my parents, who had struggled to put me through school. He had promised to help me redeploy, but six months had passed and I had heard nothing. I had come to realize that it was useless to rely on empty promises, and better to focus on my projects and make something meaningful out of my service year.

After the fuel subsidy strike I was called from the secretariat to collect approval to commence my water project. I drew out a strategy on how to get resources from ministries, parastatals and individuals. I was optimistic the project would be a success.

Often on weekends, other corps members would spend time at the lodge. We would relax and have fun. One night we had slept late, and at 2:45am we heard a loud bang. There was smoke everywhere and our windows were shattered. We woke up and ran out of our rooms in various states of undress. The male corps members carried cutlasses and prowled around outside.

The other girls and I were gathered in the common room praying. Cynthia and Miriam cried as the broken glass fell on their bodies. I remembered the SSS number that we were given in camp to call in times of distress. I dialed the number and a male voice answered. I narrated the incident and told them our location. In fewer than five minutes they called and told me they were in their vehicle, circling the church. They told me to calm the other corps members down and that there was no problem. Cynthia had cried so much that her crying induced other girls to cry more. At about 4:30 everywhere seemed calm and we went back to sleep.

When daylight came we noticed that part of the fence was damaged. It was then that we realized that the noise we had heard was dynamite detonating, but we had thought it was further away. People began to gather at the church; even neighboring houses were affected by the explosion. Uniformed men came to investigate; we were also told that something similar took place at another church near the railway.

By this point everyone was scared. It was a Sunday and we usually had mass at 7am; those that came to church went back home after seeing the damage. The press was all around asking questions, but as corps members we were not to speak to them. We contacted the NYSC local government inspector, who showed up quickly with other NYSC officials. He addressed us briefly, and all of the corps members began agitating, stating that they wanted to go home. He asked us to write down our demands, and I was given the task of writing the letter. They insisted I write that we all be relocated automatically or be sent home as we did not feel safe. I suggested that we include the option of armed security men guarding where we lived. After a long period of argument, they finally agreed with my option and we all signed our names. I was in a dilemma because I did not want to leave Bauchi without achieving anything.

The villagers for whom I intended to construct a borehole called to sympathize with me when they heard the news. One thing was clear to me at this point; I was gradually deviating from doing the project because of any award but because of the dying need of this vulnerable people. Their encouragement and constant phone calls made me determine to continue with the project.

By evening we were calm and even joked about our reactions to the events of the night before: Ifeoma had brought out her olive oil and prayerfully applied it to her face, while Miriam her roommate stretched out her out hands and begged Ifeoma to give her some too.

The next morning most of us received phone calls from our parents who had heard about the events on the network news; we calmed them down. The Bauchi NYSC state coordinator as well as the bishop of the Catholic diocese of Bauchi visited and encouraged us. The police safeguarding our residence made us secure.

I soon started printing letters and proposals and sending them to relevant ministries. I shuffled between the village and fundraising meetings when I was not on duty at work. The budget for the borehole was over N600, 000 – a lot of money – but I was optimistic I could raise it. The first group of people to assist me was the army and the police. To my surprise, they received me well and were very enthusiastic. I was also referred to a prominent individual in Bauchi who hailed from my tribe. I spoke to him about my projects. He let me finish, then he asked me,

"Do you have access to good drinking water in your home town? How many boreholes are there? And you want to provide a borehole for these ungrateful people – what is wrong with you? Why are you doing this? Please stop, because it is not worth it. Write to NYSC that you cannot continue with it." He spoke at length, even though I got his point after three sentences. When he finished his long rant of advice, he handed me a N500 note. I left his office and made up my mind not to return there for any reason in the world.

SOURCING FOR FUNDS

The next morning I got a call from the former president of the National Association of Catholic Corps Members. He told me that redeployment has been granted to all corps members serving in the northern states; there have been a rumor about this and some corps members had traveled to Abuja where redeployment was granted. I had fewer than six months left of my service year, and I was working on a project that would benefit humanity: this, to me, was reason enough to stay. My cousins had heard the news of redeployment and started calling me. When I told them that I would not redeploy, they thought I was stupid.

"You were the same person crying that you did not want to go to the northern states, and now the opportunity has come on a platter of gold and you do not want to take advantage of it." Some thought that I was dating someone in Bauchi. But how would I tell the people of this community that I would not finish the project? At this point, however, the support I was getting was diminishing. I took the little funds I had to Rural Water Supply and Sanitation Agency (RUWASSA) to see if they would commence work, but they said the money wasn't enough and that their resources had already been channeled to another similar project. Despite the challenges, something within me made me feel that I did not make a bad decision in deciding to stay. The redeployment period had ended by then anyway, so there was no going back.

I was down as most of the corps members that I looked up had been redeployed and the lodge had become dull. I told some of the corps members that I did not want to redeploy because I had gotten approval from NYSC to carry on with the project. My words gave them the courage to stay and some of them were motivated to carry out a community development project of their own.

I intensified my fundraising efforts. I woke up early each morning to plan my day. I would write in my diary all the places I would visit: this was necessary because I always had a busy schedule and if I didn't write everything down, I would forget. My job as a news reporter made things easier for me. After our morning meetings, each journalist would be assigned to a story and we would go to the venue in the company car. Sometimes the places I was assigned to were the places at which I had an appointment, so I would quickly carry out my interviews and, while waiting for the other journalists, find out if my proposals had been approved.

One day, as I walked around an office where I had submitted requests for funds, I met a man. Something about his mannerisms made me think he was intoxicated. He asked me to rewrite my letter, and said that he would help me release funds that would take care of the whole project. He was very encouraging, and I was happy that my dream of leaving my footprints in the sands of time was finally becoming a reality. I quickly called one of the reporters to know if they were through with their assignment, and he told me that they were not. I asked the man, "Sir, you said you will help me realize the funds. How will you do it?"

He answered, "Like I told you earlier, go and rewrite your letter. Inflate the price of the borehole to one million naira, and I will give you one hundred thousand naira to start the work. Then we will take pictures of the work in progress and I will use the pictures to get more funding from the government. You will do your project and we will share the remaining funds, *koba ba kaba?*"

I was very uncomfortable with the idea. He had big round eyeballs and blinked every three seconds. He was gesticulating, bending his head in every direction. As he spoke, he kept moving his fingers. It became clear to me that I must leave his office. His behavior was so distracting; I could barely hear a thing he was saying.

"*Yerinya*(which is Hausa for "girl")," he said, "Do you understand?"

"Yes, yes," I replied loudly. "You have spoken well. I will get back to you soon."

"*Tohbadamuwa*," he said, meaning "no problem". I left his office hurriedly without collecting his number. I went to the army barracks. Because I was wearing my NYSC uniform, I was quickly ushered into the army commandant's office. He was a very friendly man. "Where are you from, young lady?"

"I am from Anambra State," I replied.

"Where did you school, what did you study, and what did you graduate with?"

"I read Philosophy at the University of Benin, and I graduated with second class upper honors."

"That's wonderful – you are a very smart girl and I know you have a bright future. We will support you. Drop your letter at the receptionist's office – we will definitely get back to you." I left his office and went home. His word had boosted my confidence. I slept like a baby, reassured that my dream would soon be realized.

FIRST REJECTION

It was my turn to cook for the house the next morning. I woke up at 5am and after we had prayed together, I quickly went to the kitchen to perform my duty. We cook large quantities of food, which reminded me of Christmas when all my relatives would return home and we would go to the village. It was fun but there were always much work to do, especially in the kitchen. Most of the chores were done by girls. As I was growing up, I observed that anything which brought much joy could also bring much pain. While it was good to relax when it was not my turn to cook or wash, I knew that when my turn came it would be too stressful, especially serving people. That morning we had yam.

"I want more food! You see, you girls did not shout *extra o*! If it was pap, you would be forcing us to take extra," Chinedu said to me, frowning. As he spoke he gulped down the hot yam, burning his tongue.

"You always complain – that serves you right. Or haven't you heard that you shouldn't talk while you are eating? It is a bad habit," I answered him angrily. I knew he would still respond; he had to have the last say in every argument, as though it were a competition.

"Hmmm – see the way you are talking to me as if you are my mother. You are not my mum o!"

Frank added, "You ladies should be treating us well in this family house. You never can tell where you will find your husbands, some of us here can marry you girls o!"

Maggi, my roommate, was in the kitchen. She had been laughing and upon hearing this, she rushed to where the men were eating.

"*Na NYSC money una wan take marry wife? Abeg make una go!*" she said, mockingly. As she walked away, her wrapper shifted down revealing her thighs. She quickly tied it up.

"You see? That is what you get for making fun of us," Chinedu said to her as all the guys laughed.

"I don't have time for you guys this morning," Maggi answered, walking shamefully to the bathroom to have her bath. I hurriedly washed the pots, had my bath, and checked my diary for my appointments that day. I headed to the army barracks to find out if my request had been approved. As I collected the amount donated I said to myself, *there is hope.*

I then went to the police and asked to see the commissioner of police.

"Good morning sir, my name is Mirian. Like a daughter, I have come to seek for my father's assistance. I intend to construct the first borehole in a village of about six thousand people."

The commissioner was dressed as though he was on his way to a parade. He was a light-skinned man with fine round eyes. He did not welcome me with a smile as the commandant did, and I hesitated. I did not know what was in his mind. He looked so serious that I wondered if he would walk me out of his office.

"I just came from the office of the army commandant and he gave me his donation. That is why I have come to seek your contribution towards the actualization of this great dream of mine." I kept quiet to see if he would speak to me.

"Ok, ok," he finally spoke. "How much did the army commandant give you?"

"Well, he gave me..." My lips were shaking. Should I tell him the amount I was given? I was sure that telling him the amount would set a benchmark for his own contribution – he would give me less. I spoke up immediately: "He gave me N20,000." I felt as if hot coffee had burnt my tongue. He then opened his drawer and brought out a bundle of naira notes. "That is my donation, and I wish you all the best in your endeavor." I responded with a smile so wide that my lips almost touched my ears. I thanked him and left his office. I was having a very good day.

I went to see the deputy commissioner too; he was very cheerful and received me well.

"Take my widow's mite," he said to me. "I want you to know that even the Nigeria Police can help out." I have been following up ministries and offices but had not gotten any approvals, but the military and police had given me their contributions. I realized that sometimes we get help from places we least expect. I decided to visit the Rural Water supply and Sanitation Agency to see if they could start work with the funds I had gathered.

"*Achaba*," I shouted, and a motorcyclist rode up to me. "*Zan je Ruwassa?*" I said.

"*Na wa ki ke biya?*"

"*Naira Dari.*"

"*To muje,*" he responded. I sat on the backseat of the motorbike and we zoomed off. The speed at which the *mai achaba* took off almost made my cap fall off. I pleaded, "*dan Allah kadam kadam!*"

"*Toh! Madam ki yi hakuri!*" He reduced the speed. I looked at my face in the bike's mirror and I smiled. I imagined going into the MD's office and telling him, "These are funds I have realized. I continued looking at the mirror and smiling. The *mai achaba* saw me smiling because he was looking at his side mirror to monitor vehicle movements. He must have thought I was mad. My younger brothers often said the same after stumbling into my room to find me looking into the mirror. They could not understand why I made speeches to myself. "Girls are mysterious," my brother Obi once said to me.

I thought we must be close by now, and was shocked to look up and find that we were on the highway surrounded by desert – we were at the Maiduguri by-pass! I tried to direct the *mai achaba* but he just said, "*Shiga muje*!" Language was still a barrier, as I had only learned the basics of Hausa.

"This is not the road where I told you I was going. *Haba*!" I said.

"*Walahi, baturenshi, madam,*" he responded. It was my fault; I should have paid more attention in directing him. We finally arrived at my destination and I gave him a hundred naira.

"*kara naira hamsin,*" he said, rejecting the money I gave him.

"You asked me how much I will pay; I told you a hundred naira. You took me on the wrong route and now you want me to pay you an extra fifty naira for your own mistake?" I dropped the money on his motorbike and left. As I walked into the entrance of the building I greeted the security man at the gate.

"*Sanun ku!*"

"*Yauwa copa! Yaya yau?*"

"Lafia, yaya aiki?"

"Aiki da godiya."

I had noticed that whether at work or in the market, most people were happy when strangers made the effort to speak Hausa. I always started conversations in the language to pave my way. I saw the information officer, who took me to the MD's office. After we exchanged pleasantries, we went into the business of the day.

"Sir, I have gone round to search for funds and I have brought the little I have been able to gather so that your agency can take up the project." I spoke looking straight into his eyes.

"My dear *copa*, our agency is committed to providing potable drinking water for the various communities. Now look," he opened a file. "These are our ongoing projects. We really want to work with you but we do not have the means. We have assisted various corps members too; just go and source for more funds, we will help." He smiled as usual.

"Okay sir, I will try." I left the office and headed home to eat and sleep. I was not sad, but I was not happy either. Steve, Ayo and Ikay, who were playing Scrabble in the common room, welcomed me home.

"Well done, guys," I said.

"Welcome, o!" they replied. "This one your face is like this, hope no one looked for your trouble," Steve said.

"No one did. I just had a hectic day," I replied.

"Oh dear, go and rest before Stations of the Cross." Father Andrew, our parish priest, would get furious if any of us was within the church premises and did not attend church programs, including daily morning masses.

I went to lie down, but was soon roused by the sounds of excitement. I gave up on my nap and went to ask what was making everyone so excited. Vitalis, also known as Excess Water, ran up to me, grabbed my hands and shook them. "Mummy, have you not heard?" Vitalis was one of those that kept the house lively, but right now he was a pain in my neck. "Mummy we are going to eat big meat now, not those small cubes you ladies give us, because the bishop visited us today and gave us a big goat. Come, let me show you."

"Please, Excess Water I am tired." I struggled to regain my balance. "Please let me rest – we have an executive meeting today." Our executive meetings often lasted for hours. The Catholic corps members were very active, thanks to the former president and secretary who stayed back after their tenure to oversee another election. At last the comedian left me to take a nap.

PEER EDUCATORS' SHOCK

The cold harmattan season was gradually coming to an end. Finally I could go to bed without wearing a cardigan, and go to work without taking extra ointment to apply on the skin of my face. But the cool breeze that froze my eyes as I rode to work on the back of an *achaba* had been replaced by hot slaps of air on my cheeks.

As I had complained openly about the cold weather, I could not do so now about the heat. *Sometimes we don't know the value of what we have until we lose it*, I thought to myself. I went back to the drawing board to consider how I would complete my project as I had fewer than four months to round up my service year. I continued to visit the offices of the head of services, ministries, government boards and individuals. I submitted letters and had several follow-up meetings. One day I was at the Ministry of Youth and Sports when Mr. Sadique, one of the sports officials, introduced me to a Mr. Niyi: "My corper friend, meet this man: he knows people in this town. He will give you some links."

"Don't mind him o! I don't know anyone. I am not even an indigene," Mr. Niyi responded.

"I hear you, sir, but please help me out so that I can carry on with this project."

"Okay, I will, if you promise that you will carry out the project, because I don't want to hear that after sourcing for funds you did not embark on the project o!" he said, holding his ear and dragging it, looking at me in the eye.

"I promise I will embark on this project as soon as I realize the funds and resources," I insisted.

Mr. Niyi gave me the details of some key individuals to speak to in the various ministries. I thanked him and went on to do just as he said.

The next morning I left very early to see the states' head of Civil service. I filled the visitor's form his secretary gave to me and she ushered me in to his office. After we exchanged pleasantries, I chanted the purpose of my visit: after speaking to more than fifty people, I had memorized the statements.

"You have spoken well my dear corps member, but you will have to choose between me giving you something now and coming back during the end of the month when I can give you something bigger," he said. *A bird in the hand is worth more than a thousand in the bush*, I thought. *What if I come back next month and he begins to tell me stories?*

"Sir, I would appreciate whatever contribution you give me now." He dipped his hand into his inner caftan pocket and gave me some naira notes. I smiled as though I just won the lottery thanked him, and left his office for my community development meeting. I had been elected vice president of the Millennium Development Goals CD group and we were to have a brief meeting before heading to the various schools where we trained peer educators. I went to Federal Government College, Bauchi which was the school I had been working at. As usual, the girls ran up to me as I arrived: there was always a battle over whose classroom to use for the training. I pleaded with the girls to let me use the empty JSS1D classroom that day as we had less than an hour.

"Today, I will take you girls on the topic of assertiveness. As young women you have to say no and show that you mean it in both words and actions." I quickly ran through the lectures of the day and asked for questions. Amina, with her bright eyes and full eyelashes, was the first to raise her hand. "Aunty, you keep teaching us to say no. If we keep saying no to men, we will have no boyfriend and when it is time for marriage, we will have no husband. My aunty at home always says that men are scarce o! So we have to do whatever we can to save our relationships."

"That is true," another girl said, and all the girls started clapping and hitting their desks, praising Amina for her question. I had not anticipated such a question – the training guide had no answer. I remembered back in secondary school when my classmates and I would ask teachers naughty questions and they would rack their brains to answer. The girls clapped until they were tired and quieted down, awaiting my answer.

"I understand your worry, especially because in this part of the world the climax of a woman's success is when she is in her matrimonial home." I stopped to gather words of wisdom. "I am teaching you to say no to the pressures of premarital sex. For now, concentrating on your education is your priority. When you are fully mature, you can better judge who to spend your life with.

For now, you are too young. If any man asks you to sleep with him to prove that you love him, then you have to run away. Let me tell you a story."

I told them a story of a young girl who had a promising future because she was intelligent and got good grades at school. But when she was their age, the boys started coming and soon she became distracted. The result was pregnancy. She had an abortion at a quack hospital and died as a result of excess bleeding.

"Be the person that attracts the right people, and don't always live in fear – just be the best you can be." The whole class was quiet. I could hear the second hand of the wall clock moving. I could hear the footsteps of the teacher checking that the students were at their respective clubs. The sun went down and the atmosphere became cool. I did not know if they were quiet because I had answered their question well, but their eyes were fixed at me. For once I had gotten their maximum attention.

The bell rang and the lecture came to a close. As they walked me out, we discussed their personal issues. I took an *achaba* to the Bauchi State Television Authority to see the director of news, Mr Ibrahim and director of programs, Mr Samuel, for the leads they promised to give me, as well as to seek for advice on how to source for funds from Hajiya Fati, an influential news reporter. It was late and Aminu, a Hausa translator who often took me on his motorbike to places I didn't know in town, generously offered to give me a ride home.

PROJECT COMMISSIONING

The canopies were set up, the village women had decorated the borehole, the young and the old had gathered. The music was playing loudly and everyone was wearing their best clothes. It was a day many had died with no hope of seeing.

There were enough drinks to quench the thirst caused by the raging sun. Corps members arrived individually and in groups. They stared at the village women dancing around the decorated borehole: they had placed four wooden stands round the borehole to create a square, tied ribbons around them and placed red, white, green and yellow balloons at each angle of the square.

The invited guests and press were arriving. My father was seated under a canopy. There was joy in my heart, knowing that I made him proud. He kept smiling and looking around. I stood at a distance, imagining what it would feel like to be a proud parent. The NYSC officials arrived and the event kicked off after the opening prayer. The chairman of the occasion was the manager of RUWASSA. He gave an outstanding speech, after which it was time for me to give mine. I held the microphone and all the cameras focused on me. My hands were fidgeting, which made the paper shake. The words became double and I could not see what I was reading. It was like a dream.

I had gone to the agency a second time and still I was told to get more money. I followed all the leads I had gathered and went back the agency again, this time with the elders of the community. They tasked themselves with providing the pumps, while I sourced funds for the drilling. I succeeded in gaining more support from my place of primary assignment, individuals, ministries, corporate bodies and the government house. I went back to the agency and they finally accepted my deposit. They gave me a date when their geophysicist would go to the community to conduct a survey of the area. I was happy but scared, because the road to the village was not motorable. When I visited on my own to let members of the community know how far I have gone with sourcing for funds, the *mai achaba* often dropped me halfway in fear. I would have to call Mr. Michael or Mr. Paul, two educated residents of the community to come take me the rest of the way into the village.

The Peugeot in which the geophysicist came could not drive on the road; he and his companion came out of the car speaking Hausa. I asked what they were discussing.

"There is no road here, Madam Cofa. If this small vehicle cannot pass here, how could the big drilling vehicles?" I was furious: did this mean they would not drill the borehole? I sent a message to the village elders and they began walking down to meet us. They began conversing in Hausa. When the geophysicist saw how desperately they needed water, he was touched and walked the remaining distance.

The geophysical survey was conducted successfully and while discussing with the villagers they discovered that there was another road that they could take to reach the area.

I could hear the voice of each person, the reaction of the villagers during the geophysical survey, the children shouting, calling us *"Batore"*...and today the commissioning of the first borehole at BigiTudunwada. *If I could go through all of this and come out successfully, then why should reading a speech I wrote myself be such a tedious task?* I asked myself.

I began to speak. As I spoke, the village women kept screaming *"ayeleleleleleii"* as if they knew all that was going on in my mind. When I ended my speech, there was a loud and long ovation. Everyone was beaming.

The women called me to the center and dressed me in a local outfit they had made for me. I wondered how they got my measurements. They put a calabash on my head like those who sell *fura de nunu*, and placed a hoe on my shoulders. All of these items had my name engraved on them. The village head read his speech:

"You have built a defense for us against disaster and diseases when our well and rivers had been made undrinkable because of waste from factories. You are indeed a heroine. We have awarded you the title *Sarkin Aiyuka* and named you 'Lady Haske'. Haske means you are the real light and key of our future."

The spot where the borehole was drilled was there and then renamed "Angwan Mirian."

I was overwhelmed and could not contain my joy – all of this had come as a surprise. I had never seen people this happy in my entire life.

The moment everyone was waiting for came. The representative of the wife of the governor cut the ribbons and everyone drank from the water. I presented the uniforms and writing materials to the village students.

The journalists present took me aside: "How were you able to do this? How did you discover this village? How did you come up with initiative? "

There was a lot I did not tell them. I did not tell them this was the third time I had written a proposal to NYSC to do a project: the first proposal I wrote was to donate a transformer to a community, but I did not have enough time to achieve my goal; the second was to donate furniture to primary school pupils, but the principal did not seem trustworthy.

After commissioning the borehole, some delayed funds for the borehole was finally given to me, with the permission of NYSC I used these funds to renovate and equip a carpentry skill acquisition centre built by a corps member during her service year. My aim for renovating the dilapidated facility was my little way of meaningfully engaging the youth to reduce redundancy among them.

I had seen my posting to Bauchi as terrible news. But it turned out to be one of the best experiences of my life. It saddens me now that I and many other well-meaning Nigerians are no longer inclined to go to northern Nigeria because of the ravages of Boko-Haram. And that is indeed a tragedy. The NYSC scheme has been the only institution that acquaints Nigerians with various parts of the country—parts of Nigeria which they would never have known even existed. NYSC took me to Bauchi and got me oriented with the people and culture of northern Nigeria. It is a scheme that was well thought out and should never be allowed to fail.

This country is ours: the north, south and every cranny of it. No part should be left to itself. What affects the north, affects the south.

We must save Nigeria together.

A newspaper report on the borehole project

The well that served as the only source of water

The new borehole

Chibuzor presenting uniforms and writing materials to the head
teacher

Official opening of borehole project

A cross section of guests at the launch

A woman having a drink from the new borehole

A mother giving her son clean water from the new borehole

Chibuzor gifting school uniforms and books to pupils

The renovated Carpentry Skill Acquisition Centre

Chibuzor handing the tools to the village head

THE JOURNEY SO FAR

I could not have imagined that what started as a personal community development project was a journey to launch something more significant, a vision worth sweating for. When I returned home, family members and friends were surprised about how I came back with several recommendations, featured on TV and newspaper, from a cry cry baby to a heroine. So, I wrote The Girl Who Found Water to tell my story.

Most people felt that what I achieved was phenomenal; hence I should not stop at one borehole. Moreso, finding out that more than 60% of Nigerians did not have access to potable water, which is a basic human right, further motivated me to start a Non-Governmental Organization named Haske Water Aid and Empowerment Foundation, focusing on providing potable water and youth empowerment.

Remember Haske? I'm sure you do.

Haske was the name given to me by the people of Bigitudunwada.

We have been able to sink boreholes currently in at least 10 states in the country, and they have directly benefited more than 35 000 people. It is still a far cry as almost 60% of Nigeria's population does not have access to water, as at 2018, the president declared a state of emergency in the water sector. Part of the proceeds from this book were used to fund water project in rural communities and it attracted some partners as well.

I will not call it a walk in the park, seeing how rewarding and equally challenging the task of sinking boreholes in rural communities has been. We have faced so many challenges; even from the communities we seek to help, one sometimes wonders how the human mind thinks and functions.

These challenges, how we've been able to navigate them, and many more, I would discuss in a subsequent book.

In the midst of all these, we have also received several local and international awards for the work we're doing, and we hope to do more, one community at a time as more support comes.

So, how did we achieve these feats? How has The Girl Who Found Water, faired? What happened to the water found? How has this grown to other projects? What bigger scale of projects are we covering now? What are the challenges we've faced, and how have we surmounted them? How has it been, pushing this vision? What is the take-home for us all?

What lessons are there for corps members and others who see a need and what to do something about it? What can changemakers take home from this Journey of The Girl Who Found water?

These, and much more, I'd tell you in our sequel coming out soon...

Be on the look out!

Commissioning of Borehole project implemented by Haske
Water Aid and Empowerment Foundation, Abuja, Nigeria
2020

Commissioning of Borehole project implemented by Haske
Water Aid and Empowerment Foundation, Kano, Nigeria
2020

Other Books by the Author

Get it here:

www.chibuzorazubuike.com

Made in the USA
Las Vegas, NV
13 February 2023

67436279R00085